LEFT TO DIE

The Story of Blue Angels Leader CAPT Harley Hall

SUSAN KEEN

To: Mike
Susan Keen

HANNIBAL BOOKS
www.hannibalbooks.com

Published by
Hannibal Books
PO Box 461592
Garland, TX 75046-1592
Copyright Susan Keen 2011
All Rights Reserved
Printed in the United States of America
by Lightning Source, La Vergne, TN
Cover design by Dennis Davidson

ISBN 978-1-61315-010-8
Library of Congress Control Number 2011932288

TO ORDER ADDITIONAL COPIES SEND A CHECK FOR $14.95 PLUS $4.00 SHIPPING ($1 SHIPPING FOR EACH ADDITIONAL BOOK) TO HANNIBAL BOOKS AT THE ABOVE ADDRESS, CALL 800-747-0738, OR VISIT *www.hannibalbooks.com*

About the cover photo: Harley Hall as he gives an award in 1971. At left, collage photos, from top to bottom: the wedding of Harley and Mary Lou, August 1965; crest of the Blue Angels; Harley in the cockpit of his F-4; the Wings of Gold of a naval aviator; Harley's official Navy portrait.

Dedicated

to

Mary Lou Hall

Heather Hall and Harley Stephen Hall

What Others Are Saying about This Book:

In 1966 I was assigned from pilot training to fly the F-105 Thunderchief—a coveted assignment. My training for the 105 was at Nellis Air Force Base, Las Vegas, NV. My instructor was a man wearing a different uniform—a Navy pilot serving an exchange tour with the Air Force. He provided me with an attitude: I was to give myself no option to be anything less than the best fighter pilot to fly this big, fast, beautiful fighter called the F-105. Harley taught me never to be satisfied with good enough. He taught me to be trusted to be where I needed to be, at the place other members in my flight expected me to be— to be a professional fighter pilot. I hope Harley was proud of me. I completed my combat tour in the F-105 with more than 100 missions over North Vietnam, with three Silver Stars, three Distinguished Flying Crosses, and having saved a fellow F-105 pilot by shooting down an enemy MiG 17 that was on his tail. Yes, being a fighter pilot is an attitude, one which Harley demonstrated 24/7. He was a professional military officer—one of the best I ever knew.

David B. Waldrop, Delta Airlines captain
Pilot, U.S. Air Force F-105 Thunderchief and U.S. Marine F-8 Crusader pilot

Susan Keen has written an exceptional narrative about the unseen workings of the Blue Angels. The reader is left with an intimate knowledge of the Flight Demonstration Team while under the leadership of CAPT Harley Hall, of the history of Hall after he left the team, and of Hall's disappearance when his aircraft was shot down a few hours before the Vietnam War cease fire went into effect January 27, 1973.

Bill Pritchett
McDonnell Douglas tech representative (during the Blue Angels F-4 Phantom years)

Susan Keen's book *Left Alive to Die* chronicles the life of an up-and-coming military star. Harley Hall was the quintessential naval officer, consummate inspirational leader, and "good stick". His untimely loss—the last Vietnam shootdown—curtailed the career of an individual who would have influenced future military doctrine. A tragic loss, Harley will be remembered as a superb father, husband, professional naval aviator, and statesman.

Bill "Burner" Beardsley, Blue Angel No. 3, 1971
Delta Airlines captain (retired)

Left Alive to Die presents a brilliant and detailed portrayal of a distinguished American warrior who excelled in every aspect of his short military career. Author Susan Keen masterfully assembles the pieces to a most complex puzzle. This work finally addresses all the questions that have been raised from the time of CAPT Hall's ejection over Vietnam until his file finally was closed.

J.D. Davis, Blue Angel No. 7, 1970-71
Captain, U.S. Navy (retired)

I was privileged to be assigned to support the Blue Angels J79-8 Engines in their F-4J Phantom aircraft. Those years—working with team leaders such as Harley Hall—were the most exciting ones of my career. The Blues made me feel as if I were part of the team. Susan Keen's book, *Left Alive to Die*, documents the gripping account of Hall's last combat mission, the conflicting reports of his POW status, and the immense grief and years of determination by his wife, Mary Lou, to find the truth. A must-read!

James L. Price, Middletown, OH
General Electric factory representative, Blue Angels

This fascinating biography, *Left Alive to Die,* is much more than a thrill ride for *Top Gun* enthusiasts. The book chronicles the harrowing, devastating, and largely untold story of MIA's during and long after the war in Vietnam. *Left Alive to Die* will excite, inform, and shock the reader with its account of an almost-hidden chapter in our military history.

Bernie Hargis, producer, director, writer, and editor of television documentaries
Associate pastor, Travis Avenue Baptist Church, Fort Worth, TX

Left Alive to Die is the beautifully told, heart-wrenching story of an exceptional Naval Aviator, Blue Angel leader, and man's man. The book has all the drama, romance, and action of *The Bridges at Toko-Ri*; and it's a true story. Michener's famous line, "Where do we get such men?", was written for CAPT Harley Hall.

E. Duke Vincent, film producer, author
(as Lt. Duke Ventimiglia, a member of the Blue Angels, 1960-61)

CAPT Hall had just been assigned the position of Commanding Officer of our squadron on the *USS Enterprise* when his plane went down. He was very professional, very honest, very straightforward, and had a good sense of humor. Most importantly he was someone we could trust and follow. He was just a great aviator, officer, and gentleman. Had he lived, he would have been CNO (Admiral, Chief of Naval Operations)—no doubt about that. Hall was a Christian. On the *USS Enterprise* we talked about Christianity. He was just one of a kind; to lose people like that is a shame.

Terry Heath, wingman for CAPT Harley Hall
CDR, U.S. Navy (retired); American Airlines pilot

Acknowledgements

I owe many thanks to Mary Lou Hall and the Hall children, Harley and Heather, for their sacrifices. Mary Lou Hall's incomprehensible story reminds us that we are never to give up in our quest to find the truth. This book is written so Hall's children, Heather and Harley Stephen, who grew up without their father, will understand that CAPT Harley Hall was greatly admired, respected, loved, and appreciated by all who had the privilege of knowing him. We understand that America will remain the greatest nation on earth only as long as great leaders such as Heather and Harley Stephen's dad fight to protect it. America is only as strong as its military and its financial institutions are. If either of these fails, America will fail.

Thanks to the incredible pilots RADM Jim Maslowski, RADM Ernie Christensen, LCDR J.D. Davis, CAPT Kevin O'Mara, Steve Shoemaker, and LCDR Bill Switzer, as well as to Maintenance Officer LCDR Mack Prose, McDonald Douglas Representative Bill Pritchett, my husband Dr. Jack Keen, U.S. Navy flight surgeon responsible for providing care to CAPT Hall's Blue Angels Team and their families, and others from CAPT Hall's Blue Angels Teams who contributed to this book their stories, wealth of knowledge, and pictures. Thanks for their contributions during the Vietnam War and to U.S. Naval Aviation.

Thanks to Mark Sauter and Jim Sanders, authors of *The Men We Left Behind*, who recorded information given to them from members who were present at the Senate Select Committee on POW/MIA Affairs Hearings. Thanks also to Billy Hendon, who was on the Senate Select Committee and wrote *An*

Enormous Crime, which gives the actual POW/MIA numbers investigators presented to the committee.

As do others on the Blue Angels Teams, my husband, Jack, considers his experiences with the Blues one of the highest honors of a lifetime.

A special thanks to Camille Hornbeck, an excellent English teacher and friend. Her knowledge, skills, and dedication to detail as editor in bringing this book to fruition are very much appreciated.

Note: This book uses the following abbreviated forms (all capitals) when the author refers to a specific rank as a person's title. These reflect the style of the U.S. Navy, the branch of the military with which Harley Hall and most of the other characters in this book were affiliated. This book also follows the Navy's general style on other capitalizations of office, departments, and entities.

  ENS Ensign
  LTJG Lieutenant Junior Grade
  LT Lieutenant
  LCDR Lieutenant Commander
  CDR Commander
  CAPT Captain
  RADM Rear Admiral
  RIO Radar Intercept Officer

Contents

CDR Hall's Blue Angels Teams	11
Foreword	13
Chapter 1 "Eject! Eject!"	17
Chapter 2 "Can't Breathe!"	25
Chapter 3 Hot-Shot Naval Aviator	33
Chapter 4 Romance	42
Chapter 5 Blue Angels Leader	50
Chapter 6 Dazzling Audiences	66
Chapter 7 Top Jet Jocks	78
Chapter 8 Wild Ride	87
Chapter 9 POW Camp	96

Chapter 10
  The War at Home   101

Chapter 11
  Prisoner   109

Chapter 12
  Hall Alone   113

Chapter 13
  Down in Flames   115

Chapter 14
  Left Alive   123

Chapter 15
  Proof of Life   127

Chapter 16
  Possible Live POW/MIA Documents Shredded   140

Chapter 17
  More Documents Shredded   163

Chapter 18
  Huge Money Deal   170

Epilogue   172

References   184

Photo Album   187

CDR Hall's Blue Angels Teams

1970
CDR Harley H. Hall, USN, Flight Leader, Plane No. 1
Capt. Kevin O'Mara, USMC, Plane No. 2
LT Jim Maslowski, USN, Plane No. 3
LT Ernie Christensen, USN, Plane No. 4
LT Steve Shoemaker, USN, Plane No. 5
LT Skip Umstead, USN, Plane No. 6
LCDR J.D. Davis, USN, Narrator, Plane No. 7
LT Dick Schram, USN, Public Affairs Officer
LCDR Nelson M. Prose, USN, Maintenance Officer
LCDR Jack Keen, USNR, Flight Surgeon
LT Mary Russell, USN, Assistant Public Affairs
Bill Pritchett, McDonnell Douglas, Field Service Engineer
Ed Spinelli, General Electric, Field Service Representative

1971
CDR Harley H. Hall, USN, Flight Leader, Plane No. 1
Capt. Kevin O'Mara, USMC, Plane No. 2
LT Bill Beardsley, USN, Plane No. 3
LT Jim Maslowski, USN, Plane No. 4
LT Skip Umstead, USN, Plane No. 5
LT Bill Switzer, USN, Plane No. 6
LCDR J.D. Davis, USN, Narrator, Plane No. 7
LT Dick Schram, USN, Public Affairs Officer
LCDR Nelson M. Prose, USN, Maintenance Officer
Bill Pritchett, McDonnell Douglas, Field Service Engineer
Ed Spinelli, General Electric, Field Service Representative

CAPT HALL INSPIRED PILOTS
TO BE BETTER THAN THE BEST!

Foreword

U.S. Navy pilot. Graduate of U.S. Naval Post Graduate School. Degreed in international relations. Exchange instructor with U.S. Air Force. Blue Angels Pilot No. 1 and Officer-in-Charge. Squadron commander. Highly decorated combat veteran. Charismatic leader. Passionate aviator. Remarkable, charming, personable, handsome man. Christian. Loving husband and father. The significantly accomplished and successful CAPT Harley H. Hall stands at the center of *Left Alive to Die*, an examination of his extraordinarily larger-than-life person, stellar career, and the rippling aftermath of that fateful last mission he flew on January 27, 1973.

An insightful author, Susan Keen has penned much more than a mere biography. Moving beyond the ordinary material of many biographies Susan probes into the political machinations and government response to the POW/MIA issues which emerged during the Vietnam War. Only because of her relentless search for answers has she been able to write this gripping narrative. Countless interviews with Harley's closest friends, his wife, and his fellow aviators reveal Hall, the husband, the friend, the pilot, the instructor, the leader. Interviews with some of those involved in government investigations added to her wealth of information germane to Hall's situation. Through meticulous, painstaking research carried out on two trips to the National Archives in Washington, DC, Susan discovered horrifying facts about the status of POW/MIA's. She explores Hall's tenure with the Blue Angels, the U.S. Navy Precision Demonstration Team, and his final moments in combat. Woven into the fabric of the exemplary life of this officer are the astonishing results of the search to find truth about him and other MIA/POW's and the heart-rending, lifelong effects his shootdown had on his precious wife and children.

Susan Keen's ability to retell the story, as she skillfully integrates firsthand knowledge with her research and interviews, stems from the close association she and her husband, Jack Keen, M.D., have enjoyed with Mary Lou Hall, Harley Hall, and other Blue Angels team members and their families. During the first year Hall flew as Pilot No. 1, Keen served as the team's Flight Surgeon. Whenever the Blues were away from the home base, Naval Air Station Pensacola, Jack was with them. If any of the Blues became injured or ill, *Doc*, as they referred to Keen, served as their physician. Never the outsider, Doc was their friend and colleague; they, in turn, were his. For more than four decades these singular friendships have endured.

The glamorous stories of Blue Angels tours, dazzling performances, public acclaim, and fairy-tale marriages pale when the stark reality of this giant of a man's tragic last flight strikes home, as he is shot down over Vietnam mere hours away from the cease fire. What about his wife, whom he addressed as *My most precious Mary Lou?* Think of her: The shock of seeing the official car in front of the house. The crisply uniformed military officials standing outside the front door. The conflicting reports. The absence of concrete information.

The military wife stands unique. She functions, regardless of her husband's duty. More often than not she is the only parent present in the home, as she rears children who fear the permanent loss of a parent. Perhaps the military wife is as vulnerable to fear as are the children. She cannot allow the fear to overwhelm her. She must remain strong and calm—for the children, for the extended family, for the military spouse, for the other wives, for even the military personnel remaining on the military base. She must nurture and guide. She must perform all the household and parenting duties. What about her needs? Suppressed. Secondary. Today's oft-followed practice of "me-first" will not allow her to fill her role. During separations, whether long or short, whether training or combat (from the comforts of home the military member cannot train for the combat theater), whether unaccompanied remote assignment or naval cruise, she comforts her children and extended family. When many wives meet and marry their husbands, those men already are active-duty military. Learning to be a military wife adds another dimension and challenge to her newlywed status. Soon she knows full well the danger inherent in her husband's profession. The places in which her husband works seldom leave the background. She doesn't dwell on the dangers or the worst-case scenarios, but they are omnipresent. The role of the military wife I know. I know full well the raw fears fomented by my husband flying both in combat and routine training missions. I know the frequent separation created by frequent deployments not only for combat tours but also for training. I know the beautiful, traditional military wedding, with crossed swords overarching the happy bride and groom. I know the grand military parades and regal ceremonies. I also know the dark official vehicle, the dress uniforms of the Commander, the Casualty Assistance Officer, and the Chaplain; the heartbreaking telephone calls; the cadence of the military funeral, the boots from which emerge the inverted rifle draped with dog tags topped by green beret, the Missing Man formation fly-by, the 21-gun salute, the notes of "Taps", the tears of the Airman's, Marine's, Soldier's, or Sailor's comrades. I know these things. Mary Lou Hall knows them. I know closure. Mary Lou knows none.

Left Alive to Die does more than tell the story of a brave, courageous naval aviator and his equally brave, steadfast, loving family. The stirring pages alert us to the plight of the wives and children and extended family of men such as CAPT Hall. Masterfully told by one who knew Hall well, this compelling book reveals the glory of flying as a Blue Angel and the heartbreak of being the wife met by the official notification officers, the resulting loneliness, and the never-ending unknown.

    Camille Lee Hornbeck
    Military wife of career aviator and combat veteran
    Gold Star Mother of U.S. Army Special Forces Team
        Sergeant

Chapter 1
"Eject! Eject!"

CDR Harley Hall, handsome former commander of the Blue Angels, the U.S. Navy Flight Demonstration Team, walked across the flight deck of the gigantic carrier *USS Enterprise* and over to his F-4 Phantom. The time was around noon, January 27, 1973. Hall, the Executive Officer of VF-143, was preparing to fly his last mission over Vietnam before the cease-fire. On the flight deck he saw LCDR Ernie Christensen and waved. Christensen wandered over near Hall's aircraft.

"Boss, I guess this is it; neither of us will ever get our MiG!" Christensen, who had been a pilot on Hall's Blue Angels Team, reverted to the familiar term of respect for his former commander.[1] Christensen, the Operations Officer of Harley's sister squadron VF-142, had flown Blue Angels No. 4 on Hall's 1970 team but in 1971 returned to combat on the *Enterprise*.

"Yes, looks like we missed our chance," Hall answered. The MiG, the supersonic jet-fighter aircraft developed by the Mikoyan-Gurevich Design Bureau for the USSR and flown by the enemy during the Vietnam War, posed serious threats for American aircraft and ground troops. American crews that successfully shot down a MiG had a red star painted on the fuselage of their aircraft—one red star for each MiG. These pilots were highly revered.

Hall and Christensen talked for a few seconds more. Christensen headed back to his plane. That afternoon a quiet and growing elation of the "last real" combat mission over Vietnam underscored actions and thought. If one had been bold enough to stick his head up and look around for hope, he almost could see the end of this high-risk life—that of being a naval fighter pilot stationed on a carrier flying missions over Vietnam.

Hall climbed into his F-4 and joined his Radar Intercept Officer (RIO), LCDR Al Kientzler, who sat behind him. Kientzler was replacing Hall's regular RIO, LCDR Gary Hughes, who was Squadron Duty Officer (SDO) that day. Hall strapped in, scanned his instruments, and completed his pre-flight check.

Streaking off the deck of the *USS Enterprise*, the powerful General Electric J79 engines threw rocket-like plumes behind as the catapult in two-and-a-half seconds hurled the big McDonnell Douglas jet 300 feet through the sky at 165 mph and pinned Hall and Kientzler against the backs of their seats. For about two seconds Hall's vision, affected by the G-forces, saw a blur rather than the buttons and dials of the instrument panel. "Catapult shots feel like being shot from a cannon!" he commented over the loud engines.[2]

Hall's plane, still in afterburner, continued climbing to top speed and correct altitude to hook up with the overhead tanker and take on fuel. Over his left shoulder Hall saw his wingman, LT Terry Heath, with his RIO, LT Phil Boughton, also flying an F-4. "Taproom 113 to 114. Let's go get 'em!" Hall said over the flight frequency designated for the two-aircraft formation.

"Let's do it!" Heath, Taproom 114, answered.

After checking in with Hillsborough (the U.S. Air Force controller working northern South Vietnam) they were assigned to the Forward Air Controller (FAC) Covey 115 and directed to their target area. They reached their target at the Cua Viet River just south of the Demilitarized Zone. Then Covey 115 assigned them their mission—enemy trucks moving south from the Demilitarized Zone (DMZ). On this last day of war, communist Vietnamese troops rushed south to occupy as much land in non-communist South Vietnam as possible, while United States bombers did everything they could to stop the aggressive Viet Cong troops. Heath made his bomb run to the north, while Hall went one mile south to work a different group of trucks. Finding his target quickly Hall called in to his FAC and released his bombs.

Climbing out after his last bomb run Hall heard the dull thud of bullets or shrapnel hitting his plane. Instantly his master caution light flashed red; this indicated serious danger.

"Taproom 113 to 114. Mayday! Mayday! I'm hit!" Hall reported calmly.

"Mayday! This is Taproom 113! I'm hit! Lost PC-1 and utilities, heading feet wet!" Hall repeated.

Hall's warning light continued flashing red. His jet became a flying boulder with no maneuverability. With the tail section hit and hydraulics lost, this meant no flight control, with all hope of flying the aircraft gone. Somehow though, through sheer guts, Herculean and adrenalin-fueled body strength, and technical skill, Hall managed the jet into an almost-level position and turned east.

"Give us your position! Give us a flare—anything to tell us where you are!" Heath's backseater RIO Boughton called. Heath spotted Hall's plane two or three miles to the southeast, about 4,000 feet below. Hall's plane blazed fire from the tail section but remained flying and aloft.

"Taproom 113, I've got you! You're on fire!" Heath shouted over the radio. "Get feet wet!"

Hall needed to maneuver the plane over the water to eject so a rescue team more easily could find them. The dense jungles of the area in which Hall and his wingman were working made them vulnerable to being captured by waiting enemy ground troops. The vegetation of the jungles also prohibited clear sighting by airborne rescue operations. Landing in water also meant enemy ground troops could not capture them as easily. Thus, feet wet gave Hall and Kientzler more advantages than feet dry.

"We're trying, Terry!" Hall replied calmly. But by the second the jet became heavier and continued to fall. "Al, eject! Eject!" Hall told his backseater.

Al Kientzler yanked the face curtain, an action which set in motion the ejection sequence. This instantly fired the canopy away and ejected Kientzler through the sky. Three-fourths of a second later the rocket under Hall's seat fired. Both flyers shot clear of the plane and over water.

Heath watched as Hall and Kientzler ejected. Their plane suddenly did a roll, went into a spin, and pitched vertically— straight down to the ground.

Strong winds blew the downed crewmen away from the water; Hall's parachute was higher than that of Kientzler's. Unfortunately both men were blown west back over land to feet dry. Feet dry put them into a critical situation, since they were trying to stay over water to be rescued.

"Mayday!" Boughton called over the universal guard frequency. "Attack and radio, two F-4 crewmen are in the air!"

"Roger, I've got them," FAC Nail 89, who along with LCDR Christensen's division of aircraft had watched the ejection and crash, answered. He immediately called people to help with the rescue. Hall's plane had gone down in the target area of Christensen, whose Dakota section of F4-J aircraft was working against VC headquarters area south of the Cua Viet River. During their runs moments earlier they had received SA-7 and 37 fire. A USSR-made portable, shoulder-fired, low-altitude, surface-to-air missile, the SA-7 Grail presented threats to low-flying aircraft. Antiaircraft Artillery 37-millimeter guns posed additional threats. Christensen, who had just finished his final bombing run when he saw Hall's F-4 pass in front of him, immediately sent the remainder of his division into high holding and remained at 5,000 feet of altitude for support.

Within moments another SA-7 raced through the air. It fired straight at Heath and Boughton and went just under their plane's nose.

"Wow! That was real close!" Boughton said.

Heath descended to 3,000 feet, near the spot in which Hall and Kientzler hung from their parachutes. Heath could see that the two men looked OK, with no arms or legs missing. They still hung in normal positions from their parachutes.

"Taproom 114 Bravo, how do you read?" Kientzler called. However, trying over and over, he raised no response. Heath continued to descend to 1,000 feet, at which he saw the two chutes land about a half-mile apart. Kientzler landed first. Heath saw Hall, as soon as he landed, instantly get up and run. His parachute drifted off in the opposite direction from that of Kientzler's. Kientzler was hit in the thigh; a bullet tore through his leg and passed out the other side. This left him semiconscious and unable to run. Heath and Boughton saw that Hall and Kientzler's landing area was barren sand and dirt with few trees on an island in the Cua Viet River at the point the river empties into the Gulf of Tonkin. Visible from the air and unfortunately too visible from the ground, the two men had few chances of hiding. The area was covered with North Vietnamese troops. Heath and Boughton knew for certain Hall did get up and run; therefore, he was alive, but they weren't sure about Kientzler.

"SA-7! SA-7!" FAC Covey 115 shouted on guard; this alerted Taproom 114.

"Break right! Break right," Boughton ordered. As the backseater, part of his duties were to scan the sky forward and aft, right and left, above and below for possible enemy aircraft or missiles.

Heath quickly turned the plane right. The F-4 barely missed the SA-7 missile as it shot past their canopy. "Well, that was the second SA-7, just like they are plenty cheap!" Boughton replied.

Meanwhile Hillsborough, monitoring the guard frequency and in control of multiple aircraft ready to be assigned to bombing missions, began to vector aircraft into a holding area above the search and rescue (SAR) position. Each reported ordnance on board and time available before fuel exhaustion.

Since the shootdown was in his target area, Nail 89 was assigned SAR On-Scene Commander. "Roger, I'm on-scene commander," FAC Nail 89 answered.

Almost immediately Nail 89 radioed Covey 115, "We can't see them moving. I'm going down for a low pass to get a better fix on the situation. Cover me high; I'll be low. Stack all the other planes on top. Keep ordnance [bombs] overhead. Give me a report of any SA-7s."

"Watch your six! Been SA-7 fire here," Covey 115 warned.

"Rog, 115," Nail 89 acknowledged the warning.

"SA-7! SA-7!" Covey 115 shouted on guard.

Directly overhead of Nail 89, his FAC, Christensen, on guard frequency with Covey 115 saw an SA-7 lift and knock the tail off SA-7 Nail 89's plane—an OV-10, a two-seater spotter aircraft. End over end the plane began to tumble.

"I can't get out! I can't get out!" Nail 89 Bravo screamed into the radio.

Seconds before impact, both Nail 89 A, Lt. Mark Peterson, in the front seat, and Capt. George W. Morris, Nail 89 B in the back seat, managed to escape the aircraft. Because they were at less than 500-feet altitude, they landed almost immediately. Overhead, Christensen watched.

Peterson and Morris hit the ground. Nail 89 yelled on his

PRC survival radio, "This is Nail 89 Bravo. Looks like I'm going to be captured! Yeah, I'm going to be captured! Out!" Immediately his transmission continued, "Oh, my God! I'm getting hit! I'm getting hit! Oh, my God!"

Heath and Boughton were farther away and couldn't hear the radio transmission, because they weren't on the same radio frequency. But they did see Nail 89's plane impact. In total amazement Heath and Boughton saw Nail 89 pilots eject from their plane, their parachutes sailing above the ball of fire, but the two crew members drew heavy fire from the ground as they landed. Heath saw about 30 Viet Cong soldiers in the area looking for downed pilots and firing at Peterson and Morris as they parachuted to the ground. Nail 89's plane crashed south of the Cua Viet River, near the site on which Hall and Kientzler's parachutes landed, but not on the island. Heath and Boughton continued circling. They searched for Hall and Kientzler and the downed FAC pilots and broadcast the landing site to Covey 115. AAA and SA-7 missile fire was intense and incessant. Although flying too low to the ground was suicide, they kept looking.

Shortly after the first shootdown, *USS Enterprise* officers in the Carrier Intelligence Center (CVIC) listened as Heath and other crews scrambled to find the downed pilots. An A-6, an E-2, and six A-1E Skyraiders (Sandys) arrived; they hoped that from the downed pilots they would hear a beeper or radio or see a flare. Several times Heath and Boughton, with the Sandys, went through the clouds. They dodged AAA and SA-7 fire and pointed out the site on which Hall and Kientzler landed but saw no sign of the downed pilots. Heavily burdened in heart, Heath and Boughton returned to the *USS Enterprise*.

Recently Christensen commented, "Returning to the carrier was horrible after the terrible combat day—having seen and heard what occurred and realizing there was nothing I could do to influence their survival. I had released my ordnance and didn't have an absolute spot on the survivors. Watching people walk around in their clean, starched khakis—people who had nothing more on their minds than what the movie of the evening was going to be or when the next big mail call would take place—was surreal."

Officers on the *USS Enterprise* later debriefed Heath that South Vietnamese Bright Light Soldiers, trained by the U.S. to rescue downed pilots, reported finding Nail 89 pilots Morris and Peterson tied to a tree and decapitated. The officers received no word about Hall or Kientzler.

What happened to Hall? Herein lies the story of Harley Hall, husband and father, U.S. Navy pilot, Blue Angels Commander, Prisoner of War.

[1 & 2] Christensen and Heath furnished much of the material for chapter 1. This includes tapes of flights and debriefings.

Chapter 2
"Can't Breathe!"

Not aware of what had happened to her husband, Hall's wife, Mary Lou, was at their home in California and was preparing to attend a wedding. She and Harley were long-time friends of the bride and groom. The groom, Kevin O'Mara, had been No. 2 pilot on Hall's Blue Angels Team. The bride, LT Mary Russell (USN), was the Blues' Assistant Public Affairs Officer on Hall's team. She and Kevin began dating while Kevin was a Blue Angel and she worked in the Administrative Office. Now they were marrying, but Harley would not be there to see the ceremony.

All those involved with the day's festivities seemed to have a Blue Angel connection. LCDR Nelson (Mack) Prose, the Blue's Aeronautical Maintenance Officer, and his wife, Sandra, along with Hall's No. 6 pilot, LCDR Bill Switzer, and his wife, Pam, were picking up Mary Lou. Having already taken their daughter, Heather, to the sitter, Mary Lou now hurried to be ready when her four friends arrived.[1]

Despite the beautiful southern California day, all morning Mary Lou felt ill at ease. This was the last day of fighting before the cease-fire would go into effect at 3 p.m. Los Angeles time. Mary Lou knew that for the last few days Harley had been flying over Laos. On that day, January 27, she did not know Harley's specific location, but she urgently hoped he was completing his last mission and returning to the *USS Enterprise*. He had flown hundreds of sorties (missions), but Mary Lou did not like to think about the risk each one involved. With hundreds behind him today's would be the last. In just a few more hours the war would be ended. Six weeks earlier, in December, Mary Lou and Harley had spent a few days together in Hong Kong. Originally scheduled to last 10 days, their time together was cut short when the men were pulled and returned to combat. For much of their seven years of marriage Harley had been gone. Seven-months pregnant, Mary Lou wanted Harley at her side when their second child was born. She couldn't wait for her husband to return. At the wedding the cease fire may have weighed on all the guests' minds, but no one talked about it. Today was a happy occasion.

Seeing the radiant bride and groom at their beautiful wedding, Mary Lou, hopeful for them, felt genuine happiness. Because her own young family meant more to her than anything, she wanted everyone to be as happily married as she and Harley were. Even though every minute she missed Harley, she enjoyed the good times. Kevin and Mary's wedding counted as one of the good times.

Ironically, as the wedding ceremony ended, church bells rang all over Los Angeles to announce the cease fire in Vietnam. All the wedding party and wedding guests were so happy and excited, just for an instant they might have forgotten that this not only was Kevin's and Mary's moment, but it also was the announcement of the cease fire in Vietnam. Mary Lou, too, was happy as she walked out of the church and threw the traditional rice. The wedding reception continued the celebration of the incredible day. Guests and family took pictures, greeted the happy newlyweds, enjoyed long-standing friendships, and shared stories of times in the Blues.

On the way back to San Diego, the Proses, Switzers, and Mary Lou stopped in Escondido for Mexican food. Mary Lou was supposed to be "eating for two", as the expression about expectant moms goes, but she just didn't have much of an appetite. Reaching Rancho Bernardo, the San Diego community in which they lived, Mack and Sandra first dropped Bill and Pam at their house. As Mack drove back through the dark and deserted streets of the area which housed a large portion of Navy families, he turned onto Mary Lou's street. They noticed a dark-colored car full of people; the car was parked, with its lights out. As they drove past, the car's lights were turned on. As the vehicle began to follow them, Mack studied the car as he watched in the rear-view mirror.

"Mary Lou, let me help you into the house."

Mack pulled into her driveway, but the black car stopped in front of the house. Both knew what the car and the people in the car meant. The automobile—the dreaded black car that the Navy sent—held the four-person team of personnel that informed families of tragedy. All four individuals, dressed in formal Navy uniforms, had equally somber faces. The presence of the black car during the day was not unusual. Many military families lived in the area; for years the war in Vietnam had been raging. The number of military personnel injured, captured, and killed caused these notification teams to frequent residential areas in which military families lived. Mary Lou often followed the car through her subdivision to determine whether the vehicle would go in the direction of her house. As depressing or macabre as that type of scenario is, Mary Lou lived with the realities of war. When she married Harley, American troops already were fighting the war. He'd had two previous tours in Vietnam. To all the families thoughts of war and the black car were familiar.

When Mary Lou and Mack had walked about halfway up her front sidewalk, the four men stepped out. The men said nothing. In a moment of panic Mary Lou yelled at the men, "Well, what is it?" However, she was thinking, *I know what that car is for. They are finally here.* Did she always have an unconscious premonition? Mack had a terrible feeling in his gut. As many times as he had seen the black car, he never was ready to face whatever news the people in the car were bringing.

Mary Lou started crying as she buried herself into Mack's chest. Her tiny, five-foot frame made her head about chest high on Mack. At this point she could not say a word; she knew something had happened to Harley. Mack kept repeating, "No! Not Harley! It can't be Harley! He's such a good guy!"

The naval officers remained still; they said nothing but waited. Grim and not going away, they were present to inform, to comfort, or to help any way possible, but all the same, they stood there in front of Mary Lou and were ominously real. The tears in her eyes welled to overflowing and rolled down her cheeks. Comprehension of the reality took Mary Lou a moment. She screamed, "What has happened?"

"Ma'am, we have some bad news," began one of the men. "But it's OK. CDR Hall got out alive. He's alive. His plane went down in South Vietnam about 5:20 p.m. yesterday—about 1:20 a.m. our time. But the cease-fire has been announced; the fighting has been halted."

Mary Lou asked, "Can't we go inside?" Mary Lou realized she was very weak and about to faint. She had to sit down. "I can't breathe. I can't breathe. I have to go inside!"

Someone took her key and opened the door. The group of officers, Mack, and she went into the house. Sitting in Harley's leather chair for the longest time, Mary Lou could not stop shaking; her mind was shutting down. What the man said, these people—all this seemed unreal to her. *Harley had been through so much! How could this happen on the last possible day? The last possible mission?* Her mind was spinning. She could not stop the shaking. *This couldn't be!*

Mack was asking questions. One of the naval officers tried

to explain what he knew. "They were observed parachuting out of the plane and had two good parachutes. We know that a beeper was heard briefly. The possibility of capture is extremely high."

Mary Lou looked up. "But the first POW list was in the newspaper today. What do we do?"

"We don't know, ma'am . . .."

Mary Lou started crying again and continued shaking. Being seven-months pregnant, she knew she had to think about the baby. She looked up at the four somber officers in the room.

Mack began to speak, but another one of the officers leaned forward toward Mary Lou.

"I am your Casualty Assistance Officer, Bruce Bailey. I am here and will be here every day to assist you with all details you need. The Navy family looks after its own."

The notification team was in a potentially awkward position. Often, no member of the notification team personally knew the service member. In these kinds of situations the men and women of the team relied on paper records. Mary Lou appreciated the fact that the Commodore of the San Diego base, one of the four men present, knew Harley as a person, not just a name, rank, and serial number. Instead of offering the prescribed phrases of condolence, he used words that were comforting and meaningful.

When Mary Lou felt a tremor pass down her body, she became more afraid. "Can someone call my doctor and see what medicine I can take? I just can't stop shaking!"

Casualty Assistance Officer (CACO officer) Bailey called the on-duty physician, who prescribed a sedative.

The Navy Chaplain, also one of the four, repeated that the men were present and willing to help. Should they call anyone for her? Did she need anything?

"I just don't want to be left alone right now. I can't be alone in this house right now!"

Mack picked up the phone and called Bill Switzer, who was awakened by the call. "Bill, sorry. I am at Mary Lou's. Harley has been shot down."

"Oh, no!" Bill said, "Is he dead?"

"They don't think so. They think he was captured."

"We'll be right over!"

Mack returned to the room as the Chaplain asked, "Would you like me to call your parents or Harley's parents?"

"No, not tonight. They should not be alone when I tell them. I will have someone go to their house first before I call. I don't want to call in the middle of the night with bad news."

By this time, Mack's wife, Sandra, who had been waiting in the car, had followed the officers, Mack, and Mary Lou into the house. Sandra and Mack were newlyweds. Like Mary Lou had been when she married Harley, Sandra had no previous experience with the military and knew little of procedures or protocol. She certainly did not know the significance of the black car and its occupants at Mary Lou's house that Saturday midnight. She learned quickly. A few minutes later Bill and Pam Switzer arrived. Mary Lou was up walking and was trying to ease the shaking. She walked from room to room—walking around people, walking because she could not sit. She could barely breathe. Her entire world had just shattered into thousands of pieces. She thought, *How can life ever be wonderful again unless Harley returns home?* With her big, pregnant stomach aching she walked from room to room. If she could just throw up the Mexican food, she would feel better. Waves of nausea filled her and ran into her throat. She went into the bathroom and sat on towels near the commode. For a long time she cried and tried to throw up the food, but she never could. The sedative finally allowed her to sleep for a few hours.

When she awoke, the bad dream had not gone away. The

reality of Harley's shootdown and ejection and therefore her predicament still stared her straight in the face. *I'm seven-months' pregnant and have a 4-year-old daughter, two mortgages on the house, a car payment, and $500 in our bank account. What am I going to do if Harley doesn't come home?* She also had to make two calls—two calls that she dreaded more than anything else in the world. She had to call her parents and Harley's parents. She had to be strong for them. First Mary Lou asked her parents' best friends to go to her parents' house. At the news both her parents and their friends all went to pieces. Their friends and her parents kept asking questions she couldn't answer. *Such misery!* Next she called Harley's sister, Gwen Hall Davis, to go to the elder Halls' house so that they would not be alone when they heard about their son. When she received the call, Gwen was dressing for church. She became hysterical. Mary Lou could tell the Halls nothing more than that Harley was seen alive and thought captured by the North Vietnamese. Finally, while Mary Lou still had the strength, she called her friend who was baby-sitting Heather.

"Ruth?"

Before Mary Lou could utter another word, Ruth said, "I know. I know. We know, Mary Lou." The word of the downed plane and the news about Hall and Kientzler had spread like wildfire through the naval community in San Diego.

"Can you keep Heather today? This is not the place for her. Too many people are here. I do not want her to see this."

"Mary Lou, whatever you want me to do, I will do."

"I have to protect Heather. She is her daddy's little girl. I can't let her see this. I know I have to tell her, but not today."

"I can keep her as long as you like. Don't worry about a thing over here." Ruth, a Navy wife, felt tremendous sympathy and pain for Mary Lou and for whatever Harley was enduring at that moment.

In the days after that late-night notification, Mary Lou's house was full of people. As it would for days and days and days ahead, the phone rang incessantly. The squadron commander's wife, who had been at Mary Lou's the night before, returned early the next morning and screened the many calls. For many days afterward someone screened the calls. After the person answering repeated the name of the caller, Mary Lou gave a signal to indicate whether or not she could speak at that time. Although initially she deferred speaking with the callers, in time Mary Lou did return every single call. She recalls that while she sat in the leather chair, she felt detached, as if she were above the bustle of the household and merely was watching. At that time, Post-Traumatic Stress Disorder was unknown. A healthy mind, however, takes care of itself. Right before it breaks, the mind shuts off. On the other hand, she could not sit in the chair detached. She had to be proactive and think of her unborn child. She needed to eat properly, get adequate sleep, and maintain an active life so the baby would be healthy. Her parents, her family, and the many friends Harley and she had made helped her endure that time. Although the priest at the Episcopal church which the Halls attended knew their faces, he and the Halls did not know each other well. The family did not attend the chapel on the base, so the chaplain there didn't know them, nor did Mary Lou know him.

She did know, however, that God was with her. Her personal faith assured her that she and God could talk. That faith and her family and friends sustained her.

Right away Mary Lou's parents flew to San Diego. Her dad spent time in the kitchen cooking for the many people gathered in the house. Other people answered the doorbell and took into the kitchen food people brought. One large family in San Diego, the Navy was pulling together for Mary Lou and Harley.

[1]Chapter 2 information is taken from interviews with Mary Lou Hall.

Chapter 3
Hot-Shot Naval Aviator

From time to time as grieving people gathered at Mary Lou's house, comforting and reassuring talk gave way to reminiscences of Harley and the good times. Some two months after Hall's capture, Frank Mezzadri's ship returned to the States. Frank, who was Harley's best friend, and his wife, Suzanne, needed to see Mary Lou. They drove to her home. After the three of them cried, they talked a while.[1] Eventually Frank drifted to the kitchen and left Suzanne and Mary Lou to talk.

Mary Lou's father, Stephen J. Marino, who went by *Steve*, also was visiting Mary Lou and doing the cooking for the family as he tried to stay busy. For Steve and Frank to start talking didn't take very long. Frank wanted to talk. He was utterly dejected and distressed about Harley. Frank had kept Harley on his mind constantly since the news of Harley's shootdown and ejection into enemy territory.

Steve, a good listener, heard Frank and Harley's history together. Once more Steve was made aware of the remarkable man his daughter had married.

"So how did you meet?" Steve asked.

Frank jingled the cubes in his glass as he began his story.

"We first met while both of us were Naval Aviation Cadets training in Pensacola, but I didn't really get to know Harley until the smokers. The smokers were boxing matches between various classes. They provided entertainment for the other Navy personnel. Harley was a great boxer. The most memorable of all the matches occurred when the rest of us were standing around in the hallway outside the gym. We were trying to relax and get keyed up for our own fight. We heard roaring from the crowd inside. The noise indicated an incredible boxing match. Eventually Harley came through the door. He looked like he had been hit by a truck. Blood was all over his face.

"'Harley, what happened in there?'

"'Boy, that guy can really box! Good fighter!' Harley replied.

"'Looks like it! You are a mess. I assume the other guy won!'

"'No, I won!' Harley exclaimed.

"We became really good friends at Pensacola. Afterward we split up for advanced training. Harley went to Kingsville, TX. I went to Beeville, TX. But as fate would have it, we finished advanced training about the same time and ended up in the same squadron, VA-192. And what a reunion it was! We could not believe it! This was at Moffett Field Naval Air Station in San Francisco. We were flying A-4s."

As he processed too many memories at once, Frank looked somber for a moment,

Steve looked on, sympathetic. "San Francisco is a nice town."

"Yeah, Harley and I thought we had died and gone to heaven! Those were high times, mainly because we were in a big city. The social life available to bachelors was beyond fantastic. Life was rich and good! Moffett Field was situated at Palo Alto, just down the bay from San Francisco. We headed for San Francisco when we were not working. We were big boys! New jet jocks! We had been awarded Wings of Gold and become hot-shot Naval Aviators! We were off and running and ready to see the world!

"We trained in A-4s out of Moffett and did various deployments to Fallon, NV, and on a carrier at sea on which we earned our landing qualifications. That was a great year. Then we went on a carrier cruise together. We sailed on the *USS Bon Homme Richard*—the good ship Richard, like John Paul Jones' ship—out in the Western Pacific. Not one of the big carriers, the *Bon Homme Richard* was a smaller one but certainly good enough. We were gone nine months on cruise and loved every minute. We had shore leave when the ship docked at ports and were able to fly some."

"Was it a good squadron?"

"Yeah, VA-192, World Famous Golden Dragons, was the best squadron I was ever in. Lot of talent in that squadron—Harley and I and four of the most natural aviators I ever laid eyes on. At the time we did not realize the level of flying. One of the senior officers once said to me, 'You guys need to look around and take note. You will never be in another squadron where there is so much talent. Usually the Navy spreads it out, but you guys came in a bunch.'"

"How long was the squadron together?"

"Just the year on the *Bon Homme Richard*. Then the Navy sent us to, of all places in the world, Lemoore Naval Air Station in Lemoore, CA, in the dead-squat middle of the San Joaquin Valley. Small town surrounded by farm land. No water at all. Navy guys like Harley and I thought we would go nuts! After a year on a ship Lemoore was plenty dull. Every weekend we were off to San Francisco, San Diego, or Fresno—somewhere to relieve the boredom. And we did!"

Steve smiled. "I can just imagine."

"One time Harley and I got the idea that we would fly our A-4s from Fallon, NV, to the Pine Castle Target Range in Florida and do a little practice bombing. We were at Fallon finishing up a weapons deployment. We decided to fly the mission at low level, which meant flying without any navigational aids or instruments at all—flying low to the ground below 200 feet and off maps, stopping only for fuel. We convinced the skipper at Lemoore to let us do it!"

Frank smiled.

"While we were still in Nevada, Harley and I scheduled our target practice time and then flew out. We intended to go straight to the target range and do our simulated drop as close to the time as we could. We flew across the United States at 200 feet. We sighted off topography and towns and nailed our target in Florida inside one minute of the assigned time. We were good! Then, since we were on the other side of the country, we went to Jacksonville (FL) to refuel and headed to Boston. Boston was nice. Afterward Harley and I flew to New Orleans for a few days of R&R (rest and recuperation). We were gone four days and had a great time. We told the skipper at Lemoore that we hit our targets inside one minute of designated time. He thought we ought to call *Naval Aviation News* and get the mission written up, but we never did."

"Oh, yeah, you should have. That was a considerable feat!" Steve remarked. He was impressed with the story.

"Well, it came back to haunt us. Six months later, some other pilots from Lemoore did the exact same exercise and hit their targets within five minutes. They were written up in the press like heroes. They had probably gotten the idea from us. Problem was we just did not realize we had done anything great. We thought that was how everyone did it."

"The modesty of the gifted," Steve mused and smiled.

"Fortunately, the turnaround time between cruises was not long. Soon we were back at sea again. Same ship, same squadron, and back in Western Pacific, but now we were seasoned veterans! We knew everything! The ship was in port in Yokosuka, Japan, for two weeks. While the crews were off-loading airplanes, Harley and I used the time to do all the flying we could.

"One idea we had was to go to NAS Atsugi to get some planes to make a round-robin. We planned to circle up to the northern tip of Japan and fly back down south to NAS Atsugi. During WWII Atsugi had been an Imperial Japanese Air Base, but the U.S. Navy took it over after the war. The U.S. still has the base. Harley and I took off from Atsugi. For a while the flight north was routine. Harley was in lead position going north; however, on the trip south we planned to switch leads. A good flight. We were having fun when I noticed my fuel was suddenly running low—more like *really low*! I radioed Harley up ahead: 'Harley, what does your fuel say?'

"Harley was not having any fuel problems. He dropped back to eyeball my plane, which was streaming fuel from the back. We declared an emergency and started looking for a landing strip. We came down at Misawa, a Japanese base. A U.S. Air Force Base is there also. We landed and put the plane in line for repair, waited around for the maintenance personnel to find the leak, and then were told they did not have the part in stock. I called Atsugi to tell them the situation and that we needed a part.

"'No problem,' Atsugi said. They would fly it up to us.

"I also told Misawa maintenance we would be at the Officer's Club eating. I asked them to call us when the part arrived. After we secured the planes, in our sweaty, smelly flight suits we walked to the Officer's Club. Good thing it was an Air Force Officer's Club, as they allow flight suits in the dining room. A Naval Officer's Club would not."

Frank and Steve both smiled at this. Frank told the story with such love in his voice that Steve loved hearing it. They felt as if Harley were there with them. Frank continued:

"So we cleaned up the best that we could and walked into

37

the dining area. The waitress wisely seated us in the corner and away from the crowd. A lot of people were looking at us. Because of checking the fuel leak we both smelled a bit like jet fuel. I'm sure they could not help but notice . . . lots of officers and their wives . . . nice, polite company and half of them staring at us—a couple of Navy hot-shots stinking up the corner. Harley and I both ordered dinner. The waitress spread our meal out on the circular, four-legged table at which we were seated. We had ordered a huge meal with salad, meat, mashed potatoes, dessert, and iced tea—everything and more. At the table next to us was an Air Force major and his wife who did plenty of staring because they were within the smell zone of our flight suits. The couple was not smiling.

"Suddenly over the speaker system we heard a call, 'Either Lieutenant Junior Grade Hall or Mezzadri answer a phone call at the front desk.' The loud message got all the diners' attention. Harley started to jump up from the table to leave me there with all the disapproving looks. But when he pushed on the table to scoot his chair away, he discovered that his chair was on a rug. The table was not. So the chair didn't move, but the table did! The way Harley was pushing gave the table a little spin. The whole shebang seemed to fly into the air, all at once. It slung food in every direction possible. I don't think you could rehearse something like that . . . a once-in-a-lifetime event!

"The major and his wife, being closest, caught a majority of the mashed potatoes, gravy, and such. Most of the rest ended up on Harley and me. Harley just fell back into his chair. He was stunned! His head was spinning, I am sure. I didn't know what else to do, so I jumped up and said, 'I'll get the phone.' That at least got me out of there for a while. I was sure we were about to be lynched!

"Turns out there was a problem getting the fuel line

replacement. Atsugi would not be flying it up that night. So it looked like we would be staying in town with all our new friends. I figured we would be sleeping in the jets.

"'OK,' I told the guys on the other end of the line and started laughing. This raised questions. I had to explain how Harley managed to throw food on several high-ranking Air Force officers in the Officers' Club. Rooms might not be easy to get on short notice, but we would try. I went into the restroom at the club and tried to clean some of the gravy and pie off my flight suit and to kill time. I was going to let Harley be embarrassed as long as possible. But when I reentered the dining room, the table and mess had been cleaned up. Harley was not sitting there. I looked around for him. Harley was sitting at the table with the major and his wife, with everybody smiling and acting like old friends!"

Frank got a gleam in his eye.

"It was Harley's charm! As you know, he was a great-looking guy—always smiling—and had a very outgoing personality. He probably started off with an apology. Before long they were most likely apologizing to him for being in the way of his disaster. He just had this incredible charm! When I walked up, the major was waving me to a chair at their table. The major told me he had been talking to my friend and wanted to know the prognosis for our flight out.

"'Bad news,' I said. 'No parts tonight.'

"'Wonderful. Do you have rooms at the BOQ (Bachelor Officers' Quarters) yet? I will make a call and get two lined up for you.' The major went to the lobby to call for us. Harley's charm definitely turned the situation around. We had a very nice dinner. Later, we learned the major arranged for us a masseuse, hotsi baths, and cleaning for our flight suits. We were treated like royalty! They even pressed our flight suits with a crease in the pant legs. Harley liked this so much, he always kept his flight suit pressed with a crease in the pant leg. The next morning we got our part. When we flew out of Misawa, some of those officers turned out to give us a nice send-off. Can you believe it?"

Steve was a little misty-eyed. "So how did you two end up in the Blue Angels together?"

"Well, we were both in the Blues but not together. I went in first. We both applied for the Blue Angels after a fellow officer, CAPT Jack DeWenter, encouraged us. CAPT DeWenter had been on the Blues Team. He told Harley and me that we were exactly what the Blue Angels were looking for and that we should apply. Both of us, along with every other pilot in the Navy, wanted the prestige of being on the Navy's elite Blue Angels Team. Selection for the Blue Angels meant you were as good as any other pilot in the Navy and better than most. Harley and I applied at the same time. Before the cruise was over and before hearing from the Blue Angels, Harley was assigned to Naval Post Graduate School. This school was the move for officers headed upward as higher-ranking officers or admirals. Early on the Navy had its eye on Harley.

"Harley was assigned to the U.S. Naval Post Graduate School in Monterey, CA. He graduated in International Relations with a specialty in Middle East and Southeast Asia. For a Junior Grade Officer, his credentials were impeccable. I knew Harley really wanted to be on the Blue Angels Team; however, his being assigned to Monterey knocked him out of the tour. I told him his application was still pending. He, nor I, could never tell what might happen.

"I was in my third year as a Blue Angel when Harley finished his post-graduate work. He was stationed for a year at Nellis Air Force Base in Las Vegas with the Naval Exchange Program with the Air Force. I was with the Blues in Vegas because we were doing a couple of combined shows with the

Thunderbirds. The Thunderbirds, the Air Force equivalent of the Blue Angels, were stationed at Nellis. While I was there, I invited Harley out to the shows. At that show at Nellis, Harley met Mary Lou."

---

[1]Suzanne and Frank Mezzadri gave the information for this chapter.

Chapter 4
Romance

Mary Lou Marino, a flight attendant for Hughes Air West out of Las Vegas, frequently made the Vegas-to-Los Angeles turnaround flight, which brought her back late at night to her apartment. One such night, Lottie, Mary Lou's roommate from Luxembourg and also a flight attendant for Hughes Air West, was waiting excitedly for her. Lottie couldn't wait to share big news.

"You are not going to believe what happened today!"

"What?" Mary Lou had to know.

"Two Thunderbirds who were on my flight invited you and me to be their guests at the air show here in Vegas tomorrow. The Thunderbirds and Blue Angels will both be doing their performances here. That almost never happens. The show will be great! You have to go with me! Their shows are incredible."

"What is a Thunderbird?" Mary Lou wanted to know.

Lottie stared at her, incredulously.

"And what is a Blue Angel?"

With complete disbelief Lottie said, "You call yourself an American, but you do not know who the Thunderbirds and Blue Angels are?"

"Well, no."

"Tomorrow they are going to blow you away!" Lottie looked at Mary Lou with satisfaction. She knew her friend was about to be amazed.

"What do you mean?" Now Mary Lou was intrigued.

"I mean the Thunderbirds and Blue Angels are some of the

most amazing pilots in the world! Have you never even been to an air show?"

"No."

"OK, they fly these incredibly fast jets in formations and do aerobatic maneuvers that are unbelievable. As loud as thunder they fly just a few feet from the audience. If you have never been to a Joint Air Show at Nellis, you haven't lived! You will go, won't you? The guys are our age. Lots of them are single and so-o-o handsome, they should be on posters. I saw the Thunderbirds at the Paris Air Show when I lived in Europe and went as their personal guest. These guys are wonderful!"

"Well . . . OK." Mary Lou agreed but doubted that she would like it.[1]

She found herself sitting on wooden bleachers near the runways of Nellis Air Force Base in the bright Nevada sun. She looked at the empty blue sky and wondered what the show was all about. To imagine what an air show would be like was difficult. *Planes flying around? Is that a show? Will the experience be boring or interesting?* She saw lots of Air Force officers in the crowd and a large number of civilians such as herself. Children were there; all of them seemed to know much more about air shows than she did. The kids were pumped. Lottie was pumped. Mary Lou? Well, Mary Lou was ready for whatever when the announcer boomed over the crowd, "Nellis Air Force Base welcomes officers and their guests and all members of the public . . . ."

Every head was turned to the right. That everyone was looking for something over the eastern horizon became quite clear to Mary Lou. She looked as diligently as she could and barely made out a small bunch of dots quivering in the heat above the desert terrain. As the announcer spoke, each tiny dot grew larger. The dots turned into tiny planes that still vibrated in the heat miles away. She heard a tiny bit of a high-pitched whine.

"Officers and guests, ladies and gentlemen, it is my pleasure to introduce a combined Thunderbird and Blue Angels show!" The announcer's voice boomed majestically through the speakers.

With anticipation Mary Lou watched as the jets approached.

The jets, tightly packed together only three-feet apart, flew at high speeds through the sky and arched overhead. They made loops as they flew back down very close to the crowd and the ground. They flew rolls, dives, flips, turns, and spread into many designs—all at 600-miles per hour. Mary Lou was stunned. The smell of burnt jet fuel in the air and the rapture of the crowd were mesmerizing. She watched as the jets flew *half-an-inch apart* while they were upside down!

Like everyone else in the stands, Mary Lou was nailed to her seat as she watched throughout the entire show. Yes, these had been planes flying around as she first had wondered, but they were not just any planes and were not merely flying like a little plane with its weekend-flying owner might. These planes were flying beyond what the ordinary spectator might ever see.

After the show she was invited to meet the pilots at the party at the Officer's Club. *These guys were gorgeous!* Wearing flight suits with a Thunderbird or Blue Angels insignia, while exuding confidence and charisma, they received as much attention as any celebrity might. Everyone was so graceful and polite. Everything was beautifully laid out—the ballroom with huge chandeliers and dark wood and sumptuous food on the tables. Mary Lou was quite impressed until suddenly with no warning, one of the Blue Angels yelled, "Dead Ant!" All members of the Blue Angels and Thunderbird teams fell on their backs with legs and arms waving in the air. The handsome pilots were on the carpet and wiggled around as though they were dying ants. She did not understand. Someone had to explain the custom to her. When "dead ant" was called, at that moment the last person on the floor had to buy drinks for everyone in the room. That person became the "ant master" who was the only one that could call the next "dead ant". Even in their partying the Blues and Thunderbirds were a very competitive bunch. Mary Lou found the atmosphere and antics all very exotic. Afterward she commented to them, "I can not believe grown men behave that way! I'm from a long line of fun-loving, crazy Italians, but you men even have the Italians beat!" They all laughed. The night was great.

After she spent a three-week vacation in Europe, when she returned home Mary Lou had a phone call. "Hello! Harley Hall! Is Mary Lou there?"

She replied, "This is Mary Lou", but she wondered who was calling, because she did not recognize the caller's voice. She thought if she talked longer, maybe she could determine who he was.

"How was Europe?"

Who was this person? She gave a short answer and then asked where the two of them had met. He replied that he was a Navy pilot who met her at the Blue Angels/Thunderbird Air Show. Then he asked her out for dinner. Mary Lou could not remember him and was reluctant to go out with someone she could not remember. She was pretty sure that because he was a military officer, he had to be OK. Nonetheless, she searched her mind. The only Navy pilot she could remember who was not a Blue Angel was a guy to whom the Blues were paying a lot of attention and were crowding around. With some trepidation she accepted the invitation to dinner. She could not remember any others being at the party but was afraid one naval pilot who was as ugly as an alligator might have been off in a corner.

45

When the doorbell rang, Mary Lou opened it to find the Navy pilot in whom everyone had been so interested. He was handsome and in his coat and tie was nicely dressed. He was an easy person with whom to converse. They had dinner at a great restaurant. Afterward they caught a show at the Dunes Casino. After that first night Mary Lou knew Harley was very different from the other guys she had dated; he was very smart and very self-confident.

The next day she heard from Buster, the Thunderbird Lottie knew, who had introduced Mary Lou to Harley. Buster had told Harley about her when Harley asked at the party after the show, "Who's the cute blonde?" Buster had told Harley that she was the roommate of his friend Lottie but soon was going on a European vacation.

After their initial date Harley did call back. A whirlwind romance began. All of her friends liked Harley. Mary Lou felt quite proud to be with him. He drove a bronze Corvette that was replete with custom palomino brown leather seats and interior. He also was very good-looking. Lt. Col. Mack Angel, a Thunderbird friend of Harley's at Nellis, commented, "All the guys on the base were very glad when Harley was off the market. They also thought he was very lucky to find Mary Lou, because she was beautiful."[2]

Mary Lou did not have family in Las Vegas, so the opportunity to introduce Harley to her family did not present itself right away. Some weeks later her father called to say he had just flown into Las Vegas from Santa Barbara. He had a business meeting but wanted to have dinner that night.

"I would love to, but I have a date tonight. Can I bring him?"

"Sure. What does he do here in Vegas? Card shark?"

"He is a Navy pilot stationed in Las Vegas."

"I am having dinner with Hy Moss, a person I am doing

some real-estate business with in Las Vegas. You are not going to embarrass me, are you?"

"Dad, you will meet him when I bring him."

When he showed up, Harley was dressed in a coat and tie and looked sharp. Almost as soon as Mary Lou and Harley sat down, Harley and Hy Moss were deep in conversation about some exotic place only the two of them had visited. Neither Mary Lou nor her dad had ever heard of it. Harley and Hy became instant friends; then Harley expanded the conversation to include Steve. Before long they were talking as though they were old friends. During dessert Mary Lou saw her dad giving Harley "the look". Italians are famous for "the look". Her dad was looking intently at Harley.

The next day her dad called, "That is the man you ought to marry."

"Dad! You don't even know him. You have one conversation with him and think I should marry him!"

"I know him. Trust me; I have been around enough. I can tell a good guy when I see one."

"Well, you can just forget it. Number one, he is a confirmed bachelor. Number two, he has no intention of getting married. We have never even mentioned it. He is leaving in a year anyway. He's just here for a military exchange program with the Navy and Air Force."

"Well?"

"Well, nothing," she said. "Forget about it."

"Moss was real impressed with him, too. The boy has something special. Moss is no fool about people. I'm not either, for that matter."

Throughout the next few months her dad was in and out of Vegas. Whenever he was in town, the three of them had dinner together. As Mary Lou expected, Harley and her dad became great friends. Despite her father's knowing looks and prodding, her relationship with Harley went along in a happy-go-lucky manner. They just enjoyed spending time with each other.

On another occasion, when her father was in town, he asked the two of them to visit him in Santa Barbara. He wanted Harley to join him at his annual men's barbecue, an eccentric, boisterous ritual among a few select men and a rare invitation.

Harley never had been to such a thing but was eager to say *yes*. That Saturday through a flight club to which he belonged, Harley arranged for a small Cessna. He picked up Mary Lou for the trip to her parents' house in Santa Barbara. Mary Lou was expecting an enjoyable flight and was looking forward to getting airborne. She loved flying with Harley because he was such a confident pilot. In his hands that little Cessna flew as though it was a Rolls. Nothing could go wrong when he was at the controls, so she always felt utterly safe.

They were standing alongside the plane. Harley had just loaded their luggage when he turned suddenly and put his arms around her.

"Mary Lou, I want to marry you. Will you?"

Mary Lou said *yes*. Then everything was very exciting as they kissed and got into the plane—eventually. Once they were strapped in, Harley, more serious now, said, "I want to marry you and want us to have a great life together, but please understand that I am in the Navy. What that means is that months will go by when you are left alone. Depending on the circumstance you might even have our children alone. I am a Navy pilot; that is what I love doing. I won't get out of the Navy because you want me at home. I cannot give up my career."

"Oh, well," she said. "I will just go stay in Santa Barbara when you leave." She kissed him again.

As they taxied down the runway toward Santa Barbara, Mary Lou thought about how her life was going to change. Looking out the window of the plane, she saw houses and streets below become smaller. She was one of the luckiest women in the world. Nothing could be more perfect.

Two months later, on August 7, 1965, Harley and Mary Lou were married in a small, quaint Episcopal chapel in Santa Barbara. Theirs was a military wedding in full regalia. The groomsmen, all fellow naval officers, with their swords formed an arch under which Harley and Mary Lou walked as they left the church. In every way, with one exception, the day was perfect; her father had invited so many of his friends, for people to fit into the little chapel was impossible. The reception hall, however, had plenty of room for all the guests. Harley and Mary Lou were off to a great start!

[1] Mary Lou Hall.
[2] Mack Angel.

Chapter 5

Blue Angels Leader

After Las Vegas, San Diego was heaven. The heat in Las Vegas at times felt as if the concrete could boil water, but year-round San Diego was a temperate 65 to 70 degrees. Las Vegas, flat as a table top, was just the opposite of San Diego, in which hills covered with lush greenery rose above the Pacific Ocean. Gardens in San Diego looked as though they were jungles compared to the scrawny cacti in Vegas. All day large ships cruised in and out of the San Diego harbor.

Harley was assigned to a carrier. He and Mary Lou, however, enjoyed themselves until Harley's ship left. As planned, Mary Lou, pregnant, went to live in Santa Barbara with her parents. There their first child, Heather, was born. Fortunately, Harley returned home on schedule when Heather was 4-weeks old.

In 1969 his assignment was with the *USS Ranger* Carrier Air Wing off the coast of Vietnam. The years from 1967-68 had been his first nine-month cruise on the *USS Ranger.* In 1969 he was completing his second. Daily Hall flew missions into North Vietnam, Laos, and Cambodia. Frequently shot at, he was becoming a very seasoned pilot.

One day early in 1969 Hall was called into the *Ranger* Commanding Officer's cabin and given a message Hall had waited a long time to hear. In that unforgettable moment he heard, "Congratulations, LCDR Hall! You have orders to Pensacola as commanding officer of the Blue Angels!"

For many years Hall had applied to the Blue Angels and

had hoped for a chance to be selected for the team. Harley was very happy for Frank when Frank Mezzadri was assigned to the Blue Angels Team. Harley felt hurt, however, that the Navy sent him to school instead of giving him a Blues assignment. However, Harley never gave up; he just kept hoping. Being assigned the Blue's commander was the greatest assignment he could imagine.

"Good news, Hall. Congratulations!" The Navy officer walked out from behind his desk to shake Hall's hand.

Hall was speechless; this in itself was unusual. Then a big smile spread across his face; he saluted and said, "Yes, Sir!"

Hall was thinking he wanted to run circles around the deck, but as soon as he opened the door, he saw his squadron was standing outside. The squadron members clapped and congratulated him, as if everyone on the ship knew before he did! *Mary Lou!* Hall had to tell her the news! In Santa Barbara a Western Union messenger knocked on Mary Lou's door. Harley's wife read the message printed on the yellowish-beige, small piece of paper:

I HAVE BEEN ASSIGNED TO PENSACOLA AS COMMANDING OFFICER OF THE BLUE ANGELS! WE WILL BE MOVING TO PENSACOLA IN OCTOBER. LOVE YOU, SEE YOU SOON.

HARLEY

Mary Lou knew this assignment meant everything to Harley. Flying was his life. Leading the Blue Angels was a dream realized. She remembered his childhood story about when he looked up and saw his first plane flying overhead. Harley had been so distracted, he rode his tricycle off the porch. The experience left him with a gash on his forehead.

From that moment Harley wanted to fly. With that goal in mind he worked his way though college. Born on December 23, 1937, in Broken Bow, NV, Harley moved with his parents, Vernon and Ruby Hall, to Vancouver, WA, when Harley was about 5. He was the second of five children. The others were his older sister, Kay, and his younger siblings Gwen, Denny, and Linda. His family had insisted he not go to college but stay in Vancouver and work for Alcoa as his father had done. Harley could not explain why he could not stay, but he thought he would explode if he couldn't leave. He *had* to go to college. One day, as an underclassman on the campus of Vancouver's Clark College, where he was on the baseball team, Hall met the Navy recruiter, who told him the Navy would teach him to fly jets and would pay him to fly those high-performance machines! That was the day Hall became a Navy man. He signed up and soon was on a plane to Pensacola NAV-CADS (Naval Cadet School)—his very first flight in a plane! Mary Lou also knew how long his Blues application had been pending and how long Harley had waited for a chance to fly with the Blue Angels. But to be the leader of this group was incredible! She also was excited that he would be home and away from Vietnam.[1]

At the change-of-command ceremony in the Blue Angels Hanger, NAS Pensacola, FL, the lead officially was passed from CDR Bill Wheat to LCDR Hall. Hall became Blue Angel No. 1, Leader and Officer-in-Charge. Hall had dark hair, perfect features, and a radiant smile. With 3,700 flight hours—nearly all in fighters or attack aircraft—563 carrier landings, 169 night landings, and 11 air medals, he obtained the coveted position of Blue Angels Leader. He met the men who would be his Blue Angels Team. Three were new Blue Angels pilots who were just joining the team: CAPT Kevin O'Mara, a Marine pilot, No. 2; LT Jim Maslowski, No. 3; and LT Skip Umstead,

No. 6, solo pilot. Also new to the team was Blue Angel No. 7, LCDR J.D. Davis, team narrator and public-relations officer. At each air show Davis was responsible for flying local dignitaries and news media. LT Dick Schram, public-affairs officer, also had been on the previous team. He was responsible for advance coordination and media events; he arranged all show aspects such as show locations and lodging for the pilots and for the support personnel. Only two Blue Angels pilots remained from the previous year—LT Ernie Christensen, No. 4, who flew the slot position in the Diamond formation, and LT Steve Shoemaker, No. 5, one of the two solo pilots. They trained the new pilots. Christensen was responsible for helping the new Boss and the other two pilots on the team perfect the Diamond formation with four planes and the Delta formation with six planes.

The last few months of the year, from October to mid-December, were spent training with the current team flying over the waterfront in Pensacola. The Blue Angels assignment usually was only two years, with some of the pilots rotating off each year when new pilots joined. The 1969 Blue Angels Team had not had the best of years, because the team transitioned from using F-11 planes to a new Navy fighter, the F-4 Phantom.

Christensen explained, "Hall's reputation preceded him. He was portrayed as almost a 'water-walker'. Hall was promoted up through the ranks a year early for every promotion. At 32, when he was promoted to Commander, he was the youngest person in the Navy with the rank of Commander. From the first day I flew with Hall, he was truly a solid lead. He was great from the beginning. He had really internalized what needed to be done to hold the wingies (the planes to his left and right) in position. Hall understood the slightly positive G's on the inside (left) wingie's plane so that the wingman would never be unloaded in the turn. He equally understood the need to roll slowly enough not to cause the outside wingie on a (right) roll to have to pull too difficult to catch up with the wing. The exact roll was a very difficult thing to learn, especially in an F-4.

"From the beginning Hall understood as well that the dig his tail made (or didn't make) against the bow wave of the slot aircraft had a tremendous impact on the pull and therefore the top-out altitude and arc of a looping maneuver. No matter how tight or loose I was, relative to Hall's stabilizer going overhead, he felt it and compensated so that we got the right pull and the aircraft could truly drive the float across the top. Hall was a machine for the most part! He was so controlled and so disciplined all the way to the core. He had one of the most extraordinary abilities that I have ever witnessed to sublimate frustrations, exhilarations, disappointments, fear, and uncertainty. That ability made him so constant. And his constancy made him a solid lead and great leader."

Maslowski also spoke of the beginning of Hall's command. "At Hall's first meeting with the team in the Blue Angels Hanger, NAS Pensacola, he let us know he had the highest standards and expected the best. Nothing else would be good enough. Hall said, 'You have competed with the best. You are the winners. That is why you are here! Our mission is to represent the Navy to the public in a very positive way and to demonstrate the outstanding flying techniques that Navy pilots perform every day.'"

Hall set down new rules for how things were to be done, how the team members would behave, how they would party (which would not be like the year before), how they would fly, how they would interact, and how they would prevail. Yet he did all of this while he understood the very essential team dynamics: free flowing ideas, brutally honest briefs and debriefs, near-peer relationships, and total trust.

Hall had been at the last show of the season with the 1969 team at Point Magu. The transition began from old team (1969) to new team (1970). The previous 1969 team had had a commitment to appear on the Don Rickles Show in Hollywood, but the team members never arrived for the show. That team's missing the appearance represented a strong factor in the way Hall led the team. He made sure his team did not miss a scheduled appearance on a TV show or anything else. He was very much in control.

At the first meeting Hall told the team about a situation that occurred a year earlier. He emphasized that he didn't want a similar occurrence with this team. The previous team was practicing for a show in Kelowna, British Columbia, and was rehearsing a crossing maneuver. One of the pilots realized that No. 2 pilot Vince Donile, was going to be late for the crossover and told Donile to hustle. Donile put the jet in afterburner but didn't take it out of afterburner in time. At the crossing the aircraft broke the sound barrier and knocked out all the city windows for eight city blocks. This included windows in the mayor's office, in which the team had just received the key to the city. The mayor, understandably very upset, almost didn't let the team fly the show the next day. The Blue Angels had to plead with the mayor and promised a very safe show. Hall told the team members, "I never want to be in that position!"

Maslowski continued, "Every week we had meetings in which Hall gave his counsel, leadership, and requirements. He was the quintessential leader—towering above any other officer I have every known. But no other meetings stood out like the first one. The first practice for new Blue Angels pilots was difficult.

"As a new Blue Angel I was in utter awe on arrival at Pensacola. At 26 I was the youngest pilot ever accepted on the team and had not been flying the F-4 Phantom. They quickly put you in your proper place by adding flight training. My first training experience in Pensacola as a Blue Angel was in the back seat of the No. 4 pilot's plane. When Rick Millson came out of the chocks and began taxiing out, I thought as I looked down at the wingtips, 'Gee, these guys are taxiing out pretty close!' Then we taxied down the runway and we were still right on the wingtip. The afterburner came on and nothing changed. We roared down the runway and lifted off. The two wingtips were sitting about a foot and a half off the canopy, bouncing around. My initial thought was, *What did I get myself into?* I understood I had a long way to go to make the grade."

A few weeks after Hall took over the team as commander, one of the F-4 planes in the Blue Angels fleet had been repaired and was ready for pickup in San Diego at North Island, the big repair and overhaul facility for F-4s during the Vietnam War. Hall sent LT Steve Shoemaker, Solo Pilot No. 5 on the team the previous year, to pick up and test the plane.

North Island is on the island of Coronado in San Diego. Coronado, a very nice island, has many retired people and Navy admirals living there. Shoemaker landed at North Island and went to the hanger. Some of the men from the Blue Angels maintenance team billeted at NAS Pensacola were helping ready the plane. One of the men from the Blues asked Shoemaker whether a friend with whom he worked at the hanger at North Island could ride in the plane for the test flight.

"OK, no problem," Shoemaker answered.

So with the young guy in his back seat, Shoemaker blasted off North Island and flew to NAF El Centro, at which the Blues practice during Winter Training. Shoemaker put the plane through a series of maneuvers the solo pilots fly to check out a plane. If the plane can withstand the rigors of the solo routine, the jet should be fine for the shows.

Shoemaker finished the test and flew back to San Diego. He checked in with approach control. Control gave him a visual rather than an instrument approach. Weather was perfect. The day was a nice, clear one. The ceiling was high. Control vectored him back around to land at North Island. He never had flown in or out of North Island before, but many times he had flown out of nearby Miramar. He knew that area well. As Shoemaker approached the landing strip, he contacted flight control, the tower, to ask permission to fly a Blue Angels maneuver—one in which the plane flies at a lower-than-normal altitude at higher than normal speed and included a break, a hard turn of 180 degrees. No doubt Shoemaker knew this maneuver wasn't sanctioned in a populated area.

"I need a Blue Angels low break."

"That's approved," the tower affirmed. *Amazing!*

Shoemaker flew down the beach about 50 feet above the beach. He was clocking about 450 knots (517.5 miles per hour) and passing over the Hotel Del Coronado. He looked right at the hotel and thought, *Well, this view is interesting!* He did his break, landed, and taxied into the hanger.

"Is the plane A-OK?" Charlie Shank, the Blue Angels maintenance man, asked.

"Yes."

"We'll have it ready for you to fly back to Pensacola tomorrow morning."

LT Shoemaker picked up a rental car and met some old buddies. He showed up the next morning at base operations; he was ready to file the flight plan and take the plane back to Pensacola.

A LCDR friend of Shoemaker's who was the Operations Duty Officer of the Day said, "Steve, you better get that blue flight suit and that blue airplane and get the heck out of town as fast as you can. They are up in arms about your low break, fast-speed flying down the beach at Coronado. The phone has been ringing off the hook for 12 hours."

"OK, good idea!" Shoemaker said.

Shoemaker recalled that he climbed into the plane, strapped in, got out of Dodge real fast, and flew back to Pensacola. Retired naval people and admirals were calling the San Diego admiral, who immediately called the Pensacola admiral in charge of the Blue Angels. "You have to do something about this loud, crazy Blue Angel!" the California-based admiral demanded. Consequently, the Pensacola admiral became furious.

When Shoemaker went to work the next Monday, Hall told him, "We've got to go see the Three Star. Why don't you tell me what happened?"

"I just did a normal low Blue Angels break."

"Did you go down the beach flying real fast?"

"Well, yeah."

"They are all upset in San Diego and called the Admiral here. We have to go see him . . . NOW!"

Luckily, before they reached his office, something important had called the Admiral away. Hall and Shoemaker sat down with the Chief of Staff, a Captain. He started chewing on LT Shoemaker.

After Hall talked a bit to the Captain, the Captain said, "OK, I'll take care of it with the Admiral. No problem!"

"That episode was my first look at how great LCDR Hall really was as a leader and my first impression of him. Hall stood up for me and smoothed it all over," Shoemaker remembers. "He earned instant respect and trust from me. Here was a guy who had just been assigned as Blue Angels Leader for maybe a month. Not meaning to, I could get him and myself into a lot of trouble. But that was the way he operated. He was nonflappable: calm, cool, composed. He could talk to and was respected by the Brass, yet was one of the guys, too. He earned an A+ from me that day and became my hero," LT Shoemaker averred.

The team relocated in El Centro, CA, for Winter Training. Winter Training for the new season was intense and very difficult. No other words exist for the experience. In the F-4, if a pilot were a new pilot on the team, as O'Mara, Maslowski, and Hall were, the difficulty did not just lie in learning the maneuvers. The complexity was compounded by physically adapting to the strength and endurance required to fly the F-4 in the show environment.

From January through March practices occurred twice a day. Pilots first had to learn their "G" (gravity-pull) applications. They started with a very wide separation between the aircraft; this was further apart than fleet pilots flew. Next was learning to smooth out their flying and to fly closer together. The first step—full clear—meant no wing overlap. Half clear, the second step, had half the wing of one aircraft overlap the wing of the second aircraft. Third, Hall called Diamond, a formation with the planes clustered as closely as possible, 36 inches of separation or closer—sometimes less than a foot. Next was learning to fly this close position at 500-miles per hour plus and getting the maneuvers down precisely.

Between starting at six in the morning and not finishing until four in the afternoon were 10 hours of flying, briefs, and debriefs each day, seven days a week. Flying over the desert seven days a week for two-and-a-half months with only a single day off for a barbecue with parents and family or seeing local residents made the training time even more focused, more intense. By the end of Winter Training the Blues pilots had flown as many practices as they would fly air shows during the year. In 1970 alone they flew 120 air shows.

"I can remember going over to Hall's room. He would be sitting there with his right hand stuffed into a bucket of ice water. He commented during the early days at El Centro that he could not unclench his fist when he awoke each morning. I could laugh because I had been there the year before. O'Mara and Maslowski complained about it, but I could watch their aircraft in Winter Training that year and tell when they re-trimmed between maneuvers to ease the stick pull. Harley never did that. He really gritted it out! Every morning during Winter Training he sat there with his hand and forearm jammed into the bucket of ice water," Christensen said.

One day LCDR Hall walked into Winter Training and said, "Hey, Steve, I want you to do the Dirty Loop in the shows this year."

"You have got to be kidding me! Sure, gear flaps down and a loop in the F-4 Phantom. I don't think so!" Shoemaker answered.

"Yeah! Yeah! Exactly. You can do it!"

Hall, with Christensen, took their planes into the flight area. They both flopped around for a while until they got the aircraft flaps up and the right entry airspeed. When the planes were fuel minus (less than enough fuel to return to base with adequate and required reserve fuel) and the two pilots had learned enough about what worked, they went back. Hall went to Steve. "Yeah, Steve, it will work great!"

"Hall wasn't going to ask someone else to do something he had not done first," Shoemaker avowed.

The team did include the Dirty Loop in the show. For the entire 1970 season Shoemaker did that feature. In 1970 Hall also introduced a few other new maneuvers into the show: the Line Abreast Loop, the Tuck Under Break, the Fleur-de-lis with the lead inverted, and the Farvel with the lead inverted.

"When you consider that three of the Diamond pilots were new in 1970, along with one new solo, you have to marvel that we were able to do all those new maneuvers," Christensen said.

Returning to their home base in Pensacola was great, but the schedule was almost as intense as that of Winter Training. The Blues Team was gone every weekend, March through mid-November. The team members flew home Monday evening after the Sunday show, unless the show location was close enough to fly home afterward on Sunday. The day after they returned home was their day off, but the day typically was spent doing laundry, fixing their cars, or doing whatever else needed to be done before they left again. They practiced on Wednesday, left on Thursday or Friday, and flew to the show site for check-point verification and arrival maneuvers. The shows were Saturday and Sunday with the same schedule each week, only in different cities. Sometimes the Blues performed in two cities in a single weekend. When they flew in their first Blue Angels show in Pensacola, however, they knew this grueling routine was worth all their work, practice, and long hours.
     As a large crowd gathered at the Naval Air Station Pensacola, Mary Lou sat on wooden bleachers and waited for the air show to begin. The runway stretched a quarter-mile in either direction in front of the grandstands. For the first time at Pensacola the Blue Angels were performing with LCDR Harley Hall as leader. Dressed in shorts, hats, and comfortable shoes, people ate hot dogs and sipped soft drinks and lemonade. Along with the other pilots' wives Mary Lou and her new friend, Robin, wife of the Blue Angels Narrator, LCDR J.D. Davis, sat in the middle of the stands. Three pilots on the team, including Davis, were married. Four were single.
     The Blue Angels show began in the Diamond formation, in which the four Diamond pilots put their planes in afterburner and took off directly in front of the crowd.
     The two solos flew next, with No. 5 in a 360-degree roll, right in front of the crowd, and No. 6 taking off in a straight-up vertical, as he rolled his plane 180 degrees. The noise level was

as loud as thunder! The crowd roared, clapped, and shouted. Over the public-address system LCDR Davis said, "Ladies and gentlemen, the Blue Angels are back in town! They are the Navy's Flight Demonstration Squadron. These two maneuvers are taught to all fighter pilots. If a fighter pilot is engaged in an enemy dog-fight, these tactics shown here today help him maneuver into positions so he has the tactical advantage."

The four Diamond pilots flew straight up, vertically, to 10,000 feet (approximately two miles) to start their Vertical Opener for the show. The Diamond formation rolled onto its back and began an arc toward the ground. A boy sitting near Mary Lou yelled, "Look, I see them, over there in the sky!" Then he pointed straight to a spot in the vast blue atmosphere in which the Diamond pilots had flown.

At 8,000 feet, the team began a series of rolls, loops, and half-turns. The jets traveled very fast, in a vertical-reversal position, and turned to approach each other at a relative speed of 1,200 miles an hour. They were quite close to the crowd. Then Hall spoke over the planes' in-flight intercom, the system through which he gave commands to the Blue Angels pilots.

"Break!"

In unison the planes shot outward into four different directions and then made a loop. Simultaneously, Hall ordered, "Coming in on crossing." Immediately the four Diamond pilots crossed merely 100 feet above the runway in front of the crowd—the four aircraft at minimum separation and at a relative speed of 1,200-miles per hour. Adults erupted into applause. Children sat stunned, but adults clapped until their hands were sore. The crowd alongside the runway went nuts. The boy in front of Mary Lou shouted, "Unbelievable!" The response to the Blue Angels always is overwhelming.

Next, the two solo pilots dropped out of the sky from different directions and circled in toward each other. Directly in front of the crowd, they raced right toward each other and then turned so that they passed in front of the viewing stands with their wings vertical to the ground.

Over the PA the narrator gave the explanation of the maneuver. "That was the Opposing Knife Edge Pass. The two Blues were flying at a closing speed of 1,000-miles per hour when they crossed in front. Yet they passed with room to spare—15 feet apart!"

Davis, the announcer, waited for a dramatic moment to let this information sink in.

"The McDonald-Douglas F-4 Phantom is capable of flying 1,600-miles per hour, which is a little over Mach 2!"

Two aviation officer candidates sitting in front of Mary Lou and Robin were talking. One said, "Who wouldn't want a job like that? I would love going to work if that were my job!"

The other one answered, "Everyone at the base says the new Blue Angels leader, LCDR Harley Hall, is one of the best they have ever seen. They say he is fast-tracking to becoming an admiral."

Mary Lou and Robin turned to each other and smiled. The guys had no clue that Mary Lou and Robin were two of the Blue Angels wives. They also had no idea about the massive amount of skill, time, and team practice the Blue Angels endured at Winter Training in El Centro to obtain this level of perfection.

Blue Angels pilots continued the show with other formations unique to their performances—the same formations today's teams perform. The Diamond Roll uses four aircraft. The team members in the Diamond formation fly by as loud as thunder, only a few feet in front of the viewing stands filled with people. They roll their planes over and over while colored vapor streams from the jets' wingtips. The pilots upright their planes while crowds clap and clap and clap in awe.

Blue Angels fly the Left Echelon Roll with the four Diamond planes at staggered altitudes in parallel rows. The planes stack downward and to the left in a stair-step position below the leader, who flies at the highest elevation. Together they perform rolls and loops; they remain in this same stair-step position in front of the crowd. More than any other maneuver, this one has established each of the Blue Angels pilots as being a pilot's pilot.

Blue Angels also fly the breathtaking, graceful *Fleur de Lis*. The Blue Angels, in Diamond formation, with a solo plane below and aft of the slot, enter the *Fleur de Lis* while the solo Blue Angel rolls straight ahead near the ground. The leader, No. 1, pulls the diamond into a loop. Phantoms in the wing and slot positions separate and roll individually before they rejoin No. 1. As No. 1's plane pushes up into a climb, the other F-4s separate to roll individually before they rejoin the flight lead. Then they fly straight down again past the viewing stands in the Blue Angels Diamond. Very, very, very impressive!

The two solo F-4 Phantom pilots fly some routines alone and extremely loudly. They fly the Knife Edge, in which the two solo jets approach from the opposite direction. They pass each other in front of the viewing stands with their wings vertical to the ground; thus they replicate a knife edge. They do many Horizontal Rolls as they approach from the opposite directions; throughout their entire routine they fly horizontal aileron rolls.

Then during that first show, after the dazzling execution of the various maneuvers and formations, Hall, talking to his fellow blue Angels as he had throughout the demonstration, said, "Coming left for Delta Loop." All six planes in the Delta Loop Formation did a loop high in the sky with exact precision and timing and flew down right in front of the crowd. They all were three-feet apart with colored red and blue vapor trailing from their wingtips. The planes made a turn to land. LCDR Hall launched the final set of commands,

"Stand by for gear . . .

"Gear down . . .

"Start reducing power . . .

"Chute."

All chutes opened at exactly the same moment. The four Diamond pilots landed together; the two solos followed them. (At some show sites the Blue Angels end the show in the Delta Landing Formation, with all six pilots on the runway at once. If the runway isn't wide or long enough, they land in this alternate formation.[2])

The Blue Angels' 45-minute show, the first performance of the season at their home base and Hall's first show as Blue Angels leader and pilot No. 1, was magnificently and magically precise. Over and over under his tutelage the performance had been refined. Hall successfully had introduced new maneuvers into their repertoire and in many ways improved the show.

As the young pilots climbed out of their cockpits and saw and heard the crowd's reaction, they felt a huge adrenalin rush. They had made it! Their lives suddenly, drastically had changed! They were "Better than the Best"! Their dreams were fulfilled. They truly were Blue Angels!

[1]Mary Lou Hall, Christensen, Maslowski, Shoemaker, and Davis provided material for this chapter.

[2]*Blue Angels 1970—U.S. Navy Flight Demonstration Team.*

Note: Although Harley did not graduate from Clark, the school has recognized him as one of its Distinguished Alumni. The Clark recognition calls him a member of the "class of 1957". His degree is from The Naval Postgraduate School in International Relations with an emphasis on Middle East and Southeast Asia.

Chapter 6
Dazzling Audiences

Throughout 1970 the Blue Angels flew their F-4s in 120 air shows in cities throughout the United States and Hawaii. That same year Hall, selected for the rank of Commander ahead of his peers, led the team flawlessly.

To be selected for the Blue Angels Team, one not only had to be an incredible pilot but also had to be as good-looking as a statue of a Greek god. Having the build like one also helped. The exquisitely designed and tailored flight suits with the Blue Angels crest on the right chest matched the blue and gold colors of the Blue Angels' aircraft. With his height, dark hair, and wide smile Hall fit the image.

Every part of each public appearance from aerial maneuvers to landing, raising their canopies in unison, simultaneously climbing out of their planes, and walking in formation toward the crowd was choreographed, practiced, and executed with synchronized precision. The Blues almost breathed in unison. They were teamwork perfected and personified. With the detailed yet suspense-building narrative overlay Davis provided, the performance caused the crowd to think it was watching a movie in real life. This show was the Navy's best—dollars well-spent—something of which every American could be proud.

The experience of being a Blue Angel was a heady one. After a show the six pilots uniformly stopped on a dime and simultaneously saluted as one. The crowd burst into even more applause with enthusiastic shouts and whistles. With hopes of touching them or speaking to them or having their picture taken together or perhaps even securing an autograph, throngs of people, as if propelled by a magic force, crowded around the Blues. Being a little kid at a Blue Angels show usually meant two hours of unbroken rapture. On the children's faces the joy was obvious as the kids made their way to the front of the crowd. Hall and the team paid special attention to the children.

After signing autographs, shaking hands, and being photographed from many different angles and directions by an equal number of camera-wielding fans and media members, the team headed to the debriefing room to assess the performance and to note any tiny imperfection. Although no one else might have noticed, the team knew. That imperfection became something to be rectified, practiced, and perfected before the next show time. Each precision maneuver was graded and discussed. The debriefing usually lasted about 90 minutes.

When the debriefing ended, family time began. Little Heather, at this point running, shot through the door and grabbed Harley by the leg.

"Daddy, Daddy!"

"Hello, Princess!" Harley picked her up to hug her and smiled at Mary Lou.

"Hi, beautiful," he said as he addressed Mary Lou and kissed her. After a flight, pilots have a glow—a special *something*. They have an intense focus on people and surroundings. Mary Lou looked wonderful in her sundress with small straps and with her blonde, shoulder-length hair and Florida tan. Shedding the Blue Angel and Navy stature of CDR Hall and changing into his family role, Harley's focus centered on his wife, who was slender and petite and had perfect features. As they walked away, they were a happy family. Harley held Heather in one arm and held onto Mary Lou with the other.

Outside the debriefing room, Hall's Solo Pilot No. 6, Skip Umstead, urged Hall to accompany the guys. "We are going deep-sea fishing tomorrow. You had better change your mind, Boss, and go with us. People are catching really great blue marlin and sailfish now!"

Hall smiled. "I can't do it, guys! I promised Mary Lou and Heather a day at the beach. We will see you at 'The Ranch' later. Good luck fishing!"

Hall, the Blues, their wives, and the dates of the single team members gathered for a party, a routine occurrence at "The Ranch". The house was named by the owner, a former Blue Angel who rented the house to the single pilots on the team. Parties were a Blue Angels tradition. Mary Lou liked "The Ranch" for the big yard, the smell of magnolia blooms, and the soft, gentle ocean breeze. Skip's deep blue Volvo and Kevin's red Corvette usually were parked in front of the house.

The Blue Angels were steeped in tradition. Pensacola, the cradle of naval aviation, was like Blue Angels heaven. Since pilots usually were on the team for only two years until they rotated off, everyone desired to live as intensely and fully in the moment as possible and to soak up all being a Blue Angel meant. This was a chance of a lifetime! Even in a crowd of 20, any one of the six men was connected by awareness and instinct to the other five in the crowd. If a siren sounded, they all immediately moved together as a unit. By intuition they could do it in a flash. Through and through The Blues were a team, even when they relaxed or enjoyed time away from work.

CDR Hall's team was exceptional. By general consensus the team never had performed so well or looked so good. The Blue Angels had traveled throughout the United States and many places overseas. They had flown out of various military bases and municipal fields; they always electrified their audiences. Hall and the Blues met mayors, governors, celebrities, and everyday people. Everywhere the pilots went, people wanted to meet them. Hall even was on national TV—the

Regis Philbin Show. The commander gave a high spin to the Blue Angels and looked drop-dead gorgeous in his uniform.[1] After the incredible shows, in every city the Blue Angels were treated as though they were royalty, with parties and special events such as a luau in Hawaii and dinner on a yacht that cruised across a lake in Canada.

One of the biggest shows in 1970 was the one on Waikiki Beach on Oahu, Hawaii. The Florida-to-Hawaii flight of 2,300 miles required numerous in-flight refuelings and primarily occurred over water. Because of concerns about the transoceanic flight the Blue Angels reviewed their water-rescue procedures. If a plane malfunctioned, the pilot might have to eject (use a parachute to leave the aircraft). Hall wanted the necessary rescue procedures practiced and in place. As was his usual custom, in all things Hall required perfection and got it. During the reviews over and over he told his pilots, "If something goes wrong, don't worry about getting out of the plane or abandoning the plane. Worry about what happens after that. You could be in the water eight hours or more."[2]

And it happened—something went wrong. During the flight Plane No. 6's engine indicator light illuminated. The pilot, however, landed safely at the Marine Corps Air Station, Kaneohe, on the other side of Oahu. The Blues' maintenance team assessed and tested plane No. 6; it found and corrected the problem. Many times the maintenance crew worked until dawn so that the planes were ready to fly at the next day's show.

In a C-130 Hercules transport plane painted in Blue Angels colors the Blues brought their own maintenance crew and spare parts. The team named its C-130 "Fat Albert" for its fat fuselage and huge, cavernous capacity to carry gear and support personnel. More than 100 people were on the Blues Team, but only six of the 100 flew Blue Angels planes in the air shows. Before or after the shows Blue Angels Pilot No. 7, Team

Narrator J.D. Davis, took members of the media (newspaper, radio, television) for flights in his Blue Angels plane. On Fat Albert, along with the U.S. Marine Corps flight crew headed by pilot and co-pilot Maj. John Garriott and Maj. Anton Therriault, were members of the Blue Angels maintenance team; the team Flight Surgeon, LCDR Jack Keen, U.S. Navy Medical Corps; McDonnell-Douglas Representative Bill Pritchett; General Electric Engine Representative Ed Spinelli; and Aeronautical Maintenance Duty Officer LCDR Mack Prose. Bill Pritchett knew every inch of the plane and how each part functioned. If needed he could take it apart and rapidly put it back together and do so in his sleep. Planes always were kept in perfect condition and were ready to go at show time.[3] Like most company representatives (reps) Pritchett had access to company personnel and records that the Navy troops didn't. He could find the person with the answers for the problem. Likewise Spinelli, in his capacity as factory rep, worked as a generalist. He became the bridge between GE, the engine manufacturer, and the Navy maintenance team. Each team of support included an airframe tech rep such as Pritchett, an engine tech rep, and an avionics tech rep. The Navy Maintenance Duty Officer worked between the tech reps and his crews to oversee all repairs and the readying of planes for any type of flying slated for the day. The planes needed to be ready for a demonstration, a test run, a training mission, or a travel mission from one performance base to another.

Dr. Keen filled the slot of personal physician not only for the Blue Angels team members but also for the support personnel and families traveling with the Blues. A medical doctor specializing in flight medicine, he traveled with the team wherever the team went. He did this to ensure the pilots' health. In reality no aircrew member wants to visit with the flight surgeon, or *Doc*, as Keen was known, for personal health issues, because the Doc has the authority to put that flyer on Duty Not Requiring Flying (DNIF) status—the absolute horror for any young, healthy, testosterone-pumping jet pilot. Yet illnesses, accidents, and preventive medicine often required the oversight of a physician. Generally the flight surgeon integrated into the team smoothly and took his fair share of the kidding and joking that all the members gave to each other. But the flyers respected the flight surgeon and recognized his contributions to their mission's success. Doc (Keen) always was included in the official and off-duty activities.

Hall's demand for perfection was not limited, however, to the performances at the shows or the flights to reach show locations. He wanted everything absolutely the best for all the Blue Angels—whether they be pilot, rep, or maintenance. Before the briefings he took a helicopter ride around the show area so he knew the amount of air space and the natural barriers and land formations. Safety and knowledge were essential. Although the pilots generally stayed in hotels, the support personnel, especially the enlisted members, were billeted on base. Harley inspected these quarters to ensure they were adequate. On more than one occasion he classified the lodging unsuitable and demanded others. He took care of his people.

Performed over Waikiki Beach, the incredibly beautiful show was a picturesque performance. The gorgeous hotels lined up facing the beach and ocean. At the opposite end of the beach Diamond Head jutted into the ocean. Ocean waves crashed on the fabulous sandy beach as a few surfers rode the waves. Everyone sensed the ambiance of this lush, tropical island. The packed crowd on the beach numbered around a million eager people who watched and waited in anticipation of the Blue Angels Show. A few miles out from the center of the beach, the prime viewing area for the formations, Hall and the Blues moved into position. Standing on a platform overlooking the crowd on the beach, Davis narrated the show. Unknown to those on the ground, four jets raced their way.

As the Flight Leader, Hall called directions on his radio: "Smoke on. Water on. Up we go."

The Blues flew in from the right and held a Diamond formation. They turned on their smoke trailers and at 30-degrees nose-up altitude Hall called out orders for the next formation: "Ready . . . Break . . . Ready . . . Roll!" All four aircraft separated to roll individually in different directions while they continued their upward climb. Widely spread apart and flying inverted they reached their top position and then started the down side of the loop as they moved back into the Diamond formation. From the beach their Fleur-de-Lis formation looked as though it were a magnificent, giant flower opening up.

Ernie Christensen, Slot Pilot No. 4, coached, "Keep holding it out, Kev . . .. Bring it in, Jim." From his position Hall called another correction; step by step, using their radios, team members continuously guided each other through the maneuvers. Their voices and the commands never were heard by the crowd below.[4]

At the end of the show Blue Angels flew their planes back to the airport on the windward side of the island. The helicopter which took them to the Rainbow Hilton landed on Waikiki Beach right beside the hotel. While they sat on the sandy beach surrounded by ocean breezes, the palm trees, and the lush greenery and flowers of the Rainbow Hilton, the Blues briefed and debriefed, as they used their hands to talk about maneuvers. The next morning after their briefing for the day, they shed their swimsuits and pulled on their flight suits. Again a helicopter transported them to their planes.

The Blues were guests at a luau complete with hula dancers, orchid leis for all, much food including a whole pit-roasted pig, and tropical punches garnished with pineapple slices and orchids. Hawaiian servers dressed in leis and grass skirts walked through the crowd. Dessert magically appeared. Centered on a platter were chocolate truffles surrounded by orchids. From under the platter steam rose as if from a volcano. Another day in the life of a Blue Angel!

For this particular Blue Angels trip Mary Lou flew to Hawaii. Harley wanted her there because the show in Hawaii was one of the special shows of the year. Mary Lou was glad she joined the group. A large, magnificent fruit basket containing pineapples, bananas, mangos, macadamia nuts, fresh coconuts, and boxes of Hawaiian chocolate waited for them in their room overlooking Waikiki Beach. The pineapples, the best they ever had eaten, were much sweeter and more delicious than were those on the Mainland (continental U.S.).

The time in Hawaii was a magical one. Everything with Harley had some kind of magic. Too bad the Blue Angels assignment lasted only two or three years. To Mary Lou the clock seemed always to be ticking, because she knew Harley likely would go back to Vietnam as soon as his two-year Blue Angels assignment ended.

Each year the team flew air shows in approximately 65 different cities, with a total of four-to-six-million people watching. With Hall's leadership all air shows were incredible, but things the men could not anticipate seemed to occur.

The show in Quito, Ecuador, in 1971 became much more dangerous than they possibly could have anticipated. Quito is high in the Andes Mountains and is the highest capital city in the world. Elevation of the airfield was 10,000 feet. Surrounding the airfield the mountains, which rise up another 10,000 feet, generally are shrouded in clouds. The sites for the majority of the shows are at an altitude near sea level and offer an average of 750-square miles of open spaces in which the planes can maneuver. At this location they would be performing inside a bowl—one with mountain sides. When Hall took his customary helicopter ride around the perimeter of the show area, he was concerned about what he saw.

One Blue Angel was close to crashing into one of these mountains. O'Mara recounted, "The air show at Quito was an attention-getter! Naturally we had to be very careful, or we'd end up a fatality by flying into the mountains and clouds. So we were doing a low opener [formation]. We came in flying a trail, one plane following the other. Nos. 1 and 2 broke from the formation. No. 3 and No. 4 broke off next. Then we did a figure-eight. Instead of doing it inverted [upside down], we did a horizontal formation. A figure-eight is all a timing thing; just punch our clocks, maintain air speed, roll out on heading, and we will be able to cross fairly consistently.

"But when I looked up where I was breaking, I was heading into the mountains that were getting closer every second! My mouth was completely dry. I was perspiring more than you could believe. The weather was cloudy and raining. I had to go into afterburner just to keep inside the mountains while I pulled with all my strength on the stick. The problem in a situation like that (maneuvering in clouds and mountains) is that a pilot isn't sure where the ground is. The whole time I kept thinking to myself: *I'm going to break out any moment now; I'm going to break out, and everything is going to be all right! Yeah, that is probably the last thing the last pilot thought, just before he went into the ground!* Then I saw a little valley. I flew out of the clouds and into the valley. *Man, I got through that one! Just roll the wings level. I am happy to be alive! I'll forget about the timing, because it's blown.*

"Then inside my vision, I saw two airplanes approaching. Thinking they were the rest of the Diamond, I joined them. They were the Solos! So I ended the show as part of the solo formation instead of the Diamond. I was just happy to be alive!

The audience did not know the difference, so they all clapped.

"CDR Hall, however, not knowing what had happened to me, said, 'Well, Kevin, that entrance was different!'"[5]

In terms of audience response the show perhaps was the most successful one for that year. The Ecuadorians never had seen anything remotely like the Blue Angels or a precision flying team. Their own air force had aircraft of an earlier vintage and did not do precision flying. In their Phantoms, tearing past the people at 500 or more miles per hour in tight and rotating formations, the Blue Angels made a lasting impression. Afterward Hall and the Blues were totally mobbed by nearly a million people. The scene was almost frightening. Hall had no idea whether the crowd might be out of control like the one at an earlier show in Manila or like those at some of the shows they had done in Asia. Because the Ecuadorians loved the Blue Angels, they expressed their appreciation in nearly one-million different ways . . . just up very, very close!

A show in the eastern U.S. yielded an unexpected surrender of a fugitive. The Blues performed in a city near a densely wooded forest. As the show ended, a fugitive whom the authorities had sought surrendered. He probably thought, "Dogs and horses I can stand, but when they send military planes after me, I'm out of here. They might shoot missiles next."

In Manila, Davis, while in his plane flying a news-media member before the show, made an inverted pass. Suddenly he heard a dull thud! "Gosh, what was that?" Davis turned around. In his excitement the media guy in the back seat had pulled the handle that released the seat pan. In turn the guy had fallen out of his seat and was pressed against the canopy of the plane, which still flew upside down, fuselage belly up. Davis gingerly inverted the plane in an upright position so the guest passenger could sit properly in the back seat.

During the 1971 season LT Bill "Burner" Beardsley and

LT Bill Switzer became the two new pilots. Christensen and Shoemaker rotated off the team. LT Jim Maslowski took Christensen's place as No. 4 slot pilot in the Diamond formation. Beardsley became the No. 3 pilot in the Diamond and Switzer the new solo pilot. Beardsley tried Hall's patience.

With only three weeks left in the practice season at Naval Air Facility El Centro, Beardsley still had trouble holding the stick for the entire 45 minutes required for the show routine. The team flew with a 25-pound, nose-down trim. Burner just wasn't getting it. Hall said, "Burner, I don't care what you do. You are going to make this strike! I don't care if you tape your hand to the stick!"

The next day, flying the routine in the desert, Beardsley was hanging in there and doing fine until the vertical position. Suddenly his plane departed from the maneuver formation and flew off into the left horizon. Maslowski said, "Burner, you all right? What's going on?"

"Just a minute! Just a minute!" Beardsley answered.

Beardsley had duct-taped his hand to the stick, but during the maneuvers his hand's movement had caused the duct tape to slip. Instead of his flying in a nose-down trim position, the tape pulled the stick in the opposite direction! That evening, after the flight, Beardsley and Maslowski talked. Beardsley said, "I just don't understand why my hand gives out. How do you hold your hand?"

Maslowski demonstrated the position.

"You mean you don't cup it with your wrist so your arm is in a circular position?"

"No. Where did you get that idea?"

"Kevin taught me."

"Kevin is 6-foot-3. His arms probably could reach around the stick twice!"

On subsequent flights Beardsley dropped his arm back into

normal position. Hall was very excited that just in time for the new season, Beardsley finally got it right![6]

LT Steve Lambert had applied for the 1972 Blue Angels Team. CDR Hall called Lambert and conveyed that the Blues appreciated the fact that Lambert was an applicant for the Team but that they had decided he wasn't the guy the Blues needed. Of course Lambert was sorely disappointed. Then Hall and all the other team members started laughing and congratulating Lambert. Poor Lambert. The Blues did enjoy playing tricks on their fellow pilots.

Lambert was an instructor pilot for the F-8 Crusader at NAS Miramar. Enroute to their Far East Tour, the Blue Angels stopped at Miramar to refuel. Lambert was very excited to see CDR Hall and the Blues, especially since he had just been selected for the team. His heart was racing because he was so nervous. Hall, the first person to deplane, walked toward Lambert. Lambert saluted, "Good afternoon, CDR Hall." Hall returned the salute, walked to Lambert, reached down, and grabbed Lambert's belt buckle, a West Pacific belt buckle from a West-Pac cruise. "LT Lambert, I just want to let you know this belt buckle is not regulation."

Lambert was saluting as precisely and fast as he could. "Yes, Sir! I'll get it changed, Sir. I'll take care of it, Sir!"

"For CDR Hall, everything had to be done exactly right every day, right by the book!" Lambert remembered.[7]

Despite their antics, pranks, and good-natured joking they were tremendous showmen. Dazzling audiences was their forte.

[1]Pritchett, Mary Lou Hall, Blue Angels team members.
[2]*Threshold: The Blue Angel Experience*.
[3]*Blue Angels 1970 U.S. Navy Flight Demonstration Team*.
[4]*Threshold: The Blue Angel Experience*.
[5]O'Mara.
[6]Maslowski and Beardsley.
[7]Lambert.

Chapter 7
Top Jet Jocks

Yes, Harley Hall became the commander and leader of the U.S. Navy Blue Angels precision flying demonstration team. Before he could become a Blue Angels pilot, however, Hall first had to become a top naval aviator—a Top Jet Jock.

Naval aviators were born during World War II when planes were flown off U.S. aircraft carriers.[1] The history of naval aviation closely aligns with the events of World War II—the use of men, the equipment, and the menace of the enemy.

When Japan attacked Pearl Harbor in Hawaii on December 7, 1941, the U.S. began its participation in World War II. The attack left many U.S. ships and planes in the Pacific Fleet bombed, burned, or sunk and lying on the bottom of the ocean off the coast of Hawaii. Three U.S. aircraft carriers in the Pacific Fleet, however, were not at Pearl Harbor. The *USS Saratoga*, recently overhauled, was moored at San Diego. The *USS Lexington* was at sea about 425 miles southeast of Midway while the *USS Enterprise* (CV6) had delivered a Marine fighter squadron to Wake Island about 200 miles away and was steaming back to Pearl Harbor.[2]

The Battle of the Coral Sea was fought May 1942 with Japanese and U.S. planes flying off carriers. Previously, battleships and destroyers had been the major fighters. Because many of these ships had been rendered incapable of combat, the fighting was left to planes flying off the carriers. Although the destroyers protected the aircraft by shooting down enemy airplanes that attempted to destroy the carriers, U.S. carriers and their planes became the stars of the Navy.

Because of the success of this new breed of warrior—the naval aviator—at the end of World War II the first Blue Angels Team was formed.[3] When disinterest and lowered government funding caused his beloved Navy readiness to dwindle after the war, Admiral Chester Nimitz became alarmed. Determined to reverse this trend, he issued a directive that stated his problem. In time the message found its way to a young World War II Ace, LCDR Roy M. "Butch" Voris. (An Ace is a pilot who successfully has shot down five enemy aircraft.) Voris' written answer went back to U.S. Navy headquarters in Washington, DC. He asked to start a flight demonstration team, which soon would be a tremendous public-relations asset to the Navy. Voris soon received an official dispatch from Washington: "Proceed earliest."[4]

Voris and the three other pilots worked and trained separately from the regular training command. Their orders were to practice over the swamps of the Florida Everglades and "fly for the alligators or whatever else is out there!" After two months of practice Voris and his Demonstration Pilots were asked to fly their show for the admirals at Naval Air Station Jacksonville, FL. These men then could decide whether to keep the program.[5] Voris' team members did 17 minutes of loops, rolls, and dive-bombings. They never repeated a maneuver. As part of the demonstration they used dummies to simulate the enemy parachuting from the plane. Because the parachute on one dummy failed to open, the dummy full of sawdust and sand landed about five feet in front of the group of admirals. The dummy easily could have killed one or some of those officers! When Voris and his pilots finished the show, Voris walked over to the admiral and prepared to take his punishment. The admiral was shaking his head as Voris knelt down on his knee and assumed he was looking at a court martial. The admiral, however, merely said, "Voris, I have one suggestion. Move it out a little further on the field just in case that happens again."

With that approval Butch Voris and his fellow pilots became the Navy's first acrobatic team. The official name became the United States Navy Flight Exhibition Team. Soon this team's name was changed to the Blue Angels. On June 14, 1946, the Blue Angels flew their first air show.[6] Officially assigned to NAS Jacksonville, FL, during its existence the team has been reassigned to other bases. From Jacksonville it moved to NAS Whiting, FL, and then to Corpus Christi, TX. Finally in 1954 the team became headquartered at NAS Pensacola. The insignia for the Blue Angels first was made official in 1949.

In the formative year, soon after they finished pilot training, the team pilots were trained as demonstration pilots. They had no requirement to be carrier-qualified. Over the next 65 years, however, requirements to apply for a Blue Angel pilot slot have changed. For example, in the late '60s and early '70s pilots such as Hall needed a minimum of 1,000 flying hours in a tactical jet (fighter or fighter/attack jet), a fleet tour, and carrier qualification. Currently, a Blue Angel applicant must be a Navy or Marine aircraft carrier-qualified tactical jet pilot with 1,250 hours of tactical jet flight time and have completed a fleet tour (assignment of roughly three years that includes deployment aboard a naval vessel). Boss, the Commanding Officer who flies plane No. 1, must have 3,000 hours of tactical jet-flying time and have commanded a tactical jet squadron.

A fascination with speed and danger emerged with the incredible performances of the Blue Angels. These pilots exhibited an unbelievable mastery over their magnificent planes. People became completely hypnotized by them! The Blue Angels were the perfect public-relations attraction the Navy needed to recruit the new breed of warrior. The Navy continued to build carriers such as the *USS Enterprise*.

The *USS Enterprise* (CVN65), the world's first nuclear-powered magnificent supercarrier, commissioned in 1961, during the Vietnam War cruised the waters off the coast of Vietnam. In 1956 the older World War II *Enterprise* (CV6) had been decommissioned and sold as scrap. The new *USS Enterprise* (CVN65) could travel four years without refueling. The nuclear power eliminated the smokestacks which emitted smoke that caused corrosion on planes and parts of the ship. At the time she was built, the *Enterprise* was the world's largest carrier, with 4.47 acres of flight deck—the longest at 1,123 feet, the highest at 250 feet, and the fastest at speeds of 30-plus nautical miles per hour.[7] In any ocean of the world the *USS Enterprise* was a fantastic instant runway.

In late August 1972 the *Enterprise* deployed for Vietnam. As the ship steamed out of the San Francisco Bay, war protesters screamed insults and held protest signs. To demonstrate their distaste for the war, protesters on the Golden Gate Bridge planned to dump red paint on the aircraft.[8] The planes, therefore, were covered with plastic sheeting.

CDR Hall was the new XO (Executive Officer) of Squadron VF-143 on the *Enterprise*. Both Ernie Christensen and J.D. Davis from Hall's Blue Angels team also were aboard the *Enterprise* but in the sister squadron, Squadron VF-142.

In October the *Enterprise* arrived in the South China Sea and Gulf of Tonkin off Vietnam. The men were in time to participate in Linebacker I Operations, a joint bombing campaign carried out by the U.S. Air Force and U.S. Navy. Aircrews from the big ship stayed busy working North Vietnam before the ship sailed in mid-December to Hong Kong for an in-port period.

The *Enterprise* was "home away from home for the small city of 5,500 men aboard". A person looking at the ship would see only the top deck, which consists of runways, four

81

elevators for moving planes on and off the deck, and the island from which air controllers direct the planes. This island sits about 50-feet above deck. But not visible are the many layers of decks below the main deck. The lower decks are the ones on which the planes are stored, the men live, and the maze of compartments that accommodate ship's operations belong. Many different departments run the ship; these include executive, administration, carrier air wing, air department, combat communications, maintenance, navigation, supply, medical, dental, legal, weapons, reactor, religious, and engineering, each of which is essential for an efficiently operated ship.[9]

The Navy tries to make life aboard ship as comfortable and pleasant as possible for sailors who for months at a time live in small quarters. Food is great and available at all hours, since operating the ship and carrying out the missions assigned mean being open for business 24/7. Also, the ship contains barber shops, laundries, a post office, and ship stores at which items can be purchased. But mail call and liberty at ports of call elicit the most enthusiastic responses from the ship's personnel, who line up for these events.[10]

The *USS Enterprise* left the Gulf of Tonkin and South China Sea. It traveled to its port of call, or in-port destination, Hong Kong, and arrived around December 18, 1972. The crew members were supposed to stay in port through Christmas and head out sometime around New Year's.

Some of the wives joined their husbands. Mary Lou, now pregnant with their second child, flew to Hong Kong to meet Harley. Pat, Ernie's wife, traveled to visit Ernie. They anticipated a fun Christmas! They took in the sights, ate extraordinary meals, and were enjoying themselves when the war went high order. The *Enterprise* was ordered back on line (on duty) in Vietnam. The aircrews would be part of Operation Linebacker II, the largest bombing campaign in the entire war.

While the ship was in Hong Kong, LT Terry Heath was assigned as Hall's new wingman. Through their conversations Heath discovered a common bond that he and Hall had. Both were Christians and members of the United Methodist Church. "CDR Hall was the personification of what every great leader should be. He did not yell or scream. He took care of his people. Everyone in the squadron admired him," Heath said.

Aboard the ship each squadron had its own "ready room" in which men were briefed and debriefed for their missions. Afterward the room was more like a fraternity house; men relaxed, watched different nightly movies, received their mail from home, read the *Enterprise* newspaper, drank gallons of coffee, or played cards. They talked with other men in their squadron about many topics such as sports and current events. Always, however, they discussed the days' activities, ports of call they had visited, and what they had heard from home.

"Once, when the squadron came into the ready room, we found CDR Hall sitting in his chair with his head leaned back. He was sound asleep. Everyone laughed. They said they had never seen him go that slow before," Heath said.

In one of the early briefings Hall gave the carrier-based squadron, he provided his men this practical advice. "If you get shot down, don't act like John Wayne and start shooting at people right away. Do not get on your radio right away. The most important thing to do is to find a place to hide. Then you can communicate. As a last resort, if you have to shoot to protect yourself, then that is what you need to do."[11]

Carrier operations existed for the pilots and their planes. However, among pilots always was competition to be "Better than the Best". Pilots who obtained the honor of "Top Jet Jock" scored the highest on their carrier landings.[12]

Landing on the carrier is something about which pilots say they never become overconfident or relaxed. Carrier landings require complete and total concentration from the pilot as he operates his aircraft in the landing pattern. Whether by day or night, landing always is a hair-raising experience. Night, especially in a storm, however, is much more difficult. On a few rare occasions a pilot, having experienced a particularly difficult and frightening landing, such as landing on the carrier in stormy weather, has walked straight to the skipper's office and handed in his prized Wings of Gold—his pilot's wings. That pilot realized, "Hey, this is dangerous stuff! I could get killed!"[13]

The problems at night become significantly magnified when pilots have only pinpoints of light in which to find a horizontal point of reference on the deck. On a dark, stormy night, with the wind and rain tossing the ship about, the pilot has difficulty determining at what point the deck ends and the massive black sea begins. Both blend into one.

At night the pilot is aided by a Carrier Air Traffic Controller (CATC) on board the carrier. The CATC directs the pilot to the point at which the plane intercepts the landing glide slope. During this phase of landing the pilot operates solely with the flight instruments in the cockpit rather than with his eyes.

When the aircraft reaches a point of 1/4 mile from touchdown, the air controller transmits, "Call the Ball." At this command the pilot leaves the security of his flight instruments and immediately looks through the windscreen of the cockpit canopy out into the black inkwell as he hopes to establish an accurate visual reference while he continues to touch down. This final approach is 100-percent visual and for the pilot usually is the most difficult stage. Flying in too low may result in a "ramp strike" which, at night, is nearly always fatal for the crew. Being too high will lead to a "bolter". Then the pilot is "waved off" and has to fly around the carrier to make another approach.[14]

Even though during daylight landings pilots can see the

ship and ocean, the procedure still is difficult. Pilots land by catching the aircraft's tailhook, a hook bolted to an eight-foot bar extending from the after part of the plane, on one of the four cables stretched across the deck in a rectangular-shaped box. Pilots say that a very abrupt stop occurs when the plane catches the cable.

In the 1960s the invention of a superior light system called the Fresnel Lens Optical Landing System made landing on the carrier much easier and safer.[14] The lens has an amber light which appears at the center of a mirror. The light is, in fact, a vertical row of five lenses. To fly a perfect approach the pilot must keep the "meat ball" (amber light) aligned with a row of horizontal green lights which show the correct landing position. If the plane is too high on the glide slope, the illuminated meat ball will appear in one of the two upper lenses; if too low, the meat ball will appear on one of the lower lenses. If the pilot flies the ball correctly, he will engage the number-three wire cable and will earn himself an "OK Three" grading from the landing signal officer.[15]

When in 1970 Hall became the Blue Angels' Team Leader, he already had made 563 carrier landings and 169 night carrier landings. He had successfully first mastered the art of carrier landings and had received top scores.[16]

Naval aviators have their own magazine, *The Hook*, in which Steve B. Smith, *USS Enterprise* Aviation Ordnance Man in 1972, wrote, "I used to watch LCDR Harley Hall [on the *Enterprise*] shake the plane captain's hand off his boot as he was climbing up to the cockpit of his F-4 Phantom. I could have seen my reflection well enough to shave from his boots they were so polished . . . and so were the wings he wore and his silver oak leaves."[17] Hall wanted his uniform to be perfect, just as he wanted his flying to be perfect. That's the kind of officer and pilot he was.

[1] *Blue Angel Video.* Vincent.
[2] *A Brief History of U.S. Navy Aircraft Carriers.*
[3] *Blue Angel Video.* Vincent.
[4] Veronico and Fritz.
[5] Veronico and Fritz.
[6] Veronico and Fritz.
[7] *USS ENTERPRISE (CVN 65) The First and Finest Nuclear-Powered Aircraft Carrier.*
[8] Christensen.
[9] *USS Enterprise CVAN 65 Cruise Book 1966.*
[10] *USS Enterprise Yankee Station CVAN 65 Cruise Book 1965.*
[11] Heath.
[12] *Top Gun.*
[13] Garrison.
[14] Davis.
[15] Garrison.
[16] *Blue Angels Flight Demonstration Team.*
[17] Tannenbaum.

Chapter 8
Wild Ride

Flying an F-4 all day is utterly exhausting. Pulling G's during high-speed maneuvers can cause the blood to rush from a pilot's head and also from a RIO's and can force a loss of vision and blackouts. Standing still on earth, one's body experiences a gravitational pull of one G. If one were to accelerate fast enough to create a force of two G's, the body would weigh twice as much as its normal weight. The Blues can experience G forces as high as seven G's. To counteract blackouts or nausea Blues work out with weights to develop muscle mass in their legs and torso so they can clinch their entire bodies like a fist; this forces the blood to stay in their heads. The experience inside the cockpit during those vast spreading, double-twisting maneuvers is one of straining, groaning, and grunting to hold blood steady while the air-crew member is being shoved from side to side. The jet responds smoothly, but the pilot inside is knocked around like a pool ball. Every pilot and RIO is soaked in sweat as he steps out of an F-4.[1]

    A professional major-league baseball player, not realizing flying in a Blue Angels plane was such a tough sport, flew with the Blues. He was not able to play in his baseball game that same night. Flying with the Blue Angels was difficult for Charlie Monoxide, a Tucson radio station reporter for KLPX. He told the Blue Angels Narrator, Pilot No. 7, he wanted to fly as fast as the Blue Angels fly. He did fly that fast but eventually threw up in the barf bag tucked inside the plane. Later the reporter commented that the maneuvers, along with being upside down, were strenuous. Because the plane flew so fast in afterburner, the "trees, hills, and cacti became an absolute blur!" Similarly, Davis, Blue Angels Narrator, at air shows across the United States took local news writers and dignitaries for a "Wild Ride".[2] Newspaper articles reveal one ride usually was enough! An example is this article by Patrick Clark for the Sunday News July 4, 1971, edition of the New York *Daily News*. The article was entitled "Flight with This Angel Really a Phantom Trip".

> Navy combat pilot LCDR J.D. Davis gunned the powerful twin jet engines of the sleek swept-wing F-4 Phantom on the west field at Lakehurst Naval Air Station, making a final pre-flight check.
> The intercom in my flight helmet crackled. "O.K. Blue Angel 7. You're cleared for takeoff." I was sitting in the navigator's seat behind Davis. I was strapped securely and was comfortable, but sweat began to trickle down my sides. Nervously, I wiped my clammy palms on the olive green flight suit.
> Suddenly, I noticed what looked like steam rising up into the cockpit from a spot near my right foot.
> J.D. said: "Don't worry about that. It's condensation. When I fly, I like it cool." Then he said, "Are you ready to go, Pat?"
> I said to myself, "What the hell are you doing here?" But then trying to sound cool and maybe a little cocky, I replied: "O.K. Let's hit it."
> And hit it he did.
> It was a lightning takeoff, like a cheetah after an antelope, the Phantom leaped ahead down the 5,000-foot runway. Within seconds the thundering roar was left behind. Now just a few feet off the deck, the loudest

sound in the cockpit was a high pitched whistle of air rushing past the body of the jet.

Suddenly J.D. pulled back the stick and, in seconds, the Phantom, a kind of Ferrari with feet, was airborne and we flashed across the west field. For an instant, I felt I was sitting on the nose of an Apollo moon shot.

"This is some kind of bird," said Davis's voice over the intercom. "It's so smooth and quick to respond, you really feel free."

I agreed, but I think my voice was beginning to sound a little thin.

Next, we headed southeast out toward Atlantic City and the ocean. A front of thick clouds, a wall of cotton, was stacked up where the land met water. The wings rocketed straight up to 6,000 feet. My heart pounded, droplets of perspiration dripped from my forehead and I was sure I left my stomach somewhere on the runway. The earth still clutched me, and the powerful pull of gravity jammed me down in the seat.

Davis told me to look out the right side of the plane. The ground, falling away like a dropping rock, looked like a brown and green quilt.

Then J. D . . . leveled off the Mach 2 (1,600-plus mph), all-weather fighter-bomber. "We'll do a tactical roll now, so you get the feel of things," he said. As the jet, now moving out at about 450 mph, rolled over, blood drained from my head. Upside down I saw a blur of earth where a calm azure sky had been a moment before.

He brought the Phantom out of the roll smartly, and then began the first of three low-level passes over the airfield.

Turning and banking sharply at about 6,000 feet, the

Phantom dropped with sudden and almost terrifying swiftness, plummeting toward the runway like a hawk.

Although bound snugly in the seat, I felt my body fight the terrible rush toward the ground. As we dropped, a lightning bolt of blue and orange and silver, my stomach seemed to churn up into my tightened, very dry throat.

Again I heard the high whistle of rushing air. This time I was aware of dull crashing of the twin jet engines. Once I had ridden in a Corvette in a quarter-mile drag race. The engine sound in the jet was almost the same.

Davis called New York center on the radio for permission to perform aerobatics, a serial of aerial combat maneuvers which form part of the Blue Angels flying repertoire.

A voice said: "Roger, Blue Angel 7. You're cleared for aerobatics." The two maneuvers I remember were the first, a barrel roll, and the second, a vertical loop. The vertical loop started at about 5,000 feet. With a heart-stopping rush, straight up toward the shimmering white sun, the jet shot skyward. At about 19,000 feet, J. D. delicately nosed the Phantom onto its back. And then we fell—nose straight down.

That's when I fought off a desperate urge to throw up. Just before we had taken off, Charlie Shank, J.D.'s veteran crew chief, had pointed to a white bag atop the instrument panel and advised me: "If you start feeling uncomfortable, use this."

By breathing deeply and quickly and then focusing my eyes on the altimeter, I was able to shake off the nausea. My street clothes, which I was wearing under the flight suit, now were soaked with perspiration.

With tower clearance to land, we whipped down smoothly into a beautiful and soft, fast (130 mph) touchdown.

"That was a good one, boss," said Charlie's voice over the intercom.

We taxied back to the hangar area. Knees shaking, I climbed out of the cockpit and dropped unsteadily to the ground.

"You didn't do bad for a rookie," a Navy ground crewman said.

I turned and thanked Davis, "That was the wildest ride of my life. When can we do it again?"

But then later, I wondered if I really had meant what I said.

Another article was entitled "'Green Angel' Tries Wings With 'Blues'". It was written by Tom Allen and on July 17, 1971 appeared in the *Omaha World Herald*.

Nebraska was upside down Friday morning. There was Lincoln and the State Capitol perched on the toe of the sower atop the Capitol dome.

One second I weighed as much as 620 pounds, four times my normal weight, and the next I was nearly weightless.

One moment I couldn't raise my half-pound camera, the next it floated above my chest.

I was in heaven.

I must have been for I was an angel—if slightly greenish—flying with a Blue Angel of the U.S. Navy's famous precision flight demonstration team.

They are in Lincoln for the weekend, saluting the Nebraska Air National Guard on its 25th anniversary

. . .. This afternoon and Sunday at 2 p.m., the team led by CDR Harley H. Hall . . . will zoom their stuff for the public . . ..

I got an Angel's eye view in a special 30-minute flight at 9 a.m. Friday. My "Gabriel" was LCDR James D. Davis, 33, of Mechanicsburg, PA, a Vietnam combat veteran . . .. "These are burp sacks in there. We like to keep this ship nice and neat. Use 'em if you need to," he said.

Then just before takeoff: "Want to give you a little feel of just what it's like," he said. "If it gets too uncomfortable, holler and we'll ease up a bit."

As we started down the runway he added: "You'll feel a little kick in the pants. Don't worry. We are just kicking it up a little."

I didn't have time to worry. The altimeter needle spun like a top as we took off in a vertical climb. The Phantom climbs 9,842 feet in 34.52 seconds.

"You OK?" he asked as we parted the heavenly gates . . .. In a split second we had completed the loop and were diving straight down for the earth. Somewhere on the back side of the loop I gained 465 pounds as we reached four G's. My jaw sagged. So did my eyelids below my eyes bulging at the earth zooming toward us . . .. "Now I will show you how our astronauts feel in weightlessness," my Blue Angel chirped.

It was like coming up over the top of a roller coaster and my camera floated above my chest. "Now a negative G—it's just like standing on your head." There were vertical loops and what he called "playing around with the roll rate" as we corkscrewed through the sky . . ..

My proudest moment came when Shank anxiously

glanced at the burp bag compartment as he unbuckled my harness. "Good boy," he said with a thump on my helmet.

Allan, the "Green" Angel, had returned with stomach intact! Yet another story was written by Edward D. Williams and appeared in *The Milwaukee Journal* on July 24, 1970.

The curtain went up on the Air Show at Mitchell Field Friday. The flight showed why the team picked the Phantom, the United States' most versatile jet fighter-bomber, for its air demonstrations . . . . The powerful plane did things the team's previous plane, the F-11 Tiger, could not do. As a preview, LCDR James Davis made some three flights with one newsman in the two seat McDonnell Douglas F-4J Phantom jet on each flight. The passengers included . . . this Milwaukee Journal reporter . . . .

Davis sat in the front seat and his passenger sat in the rear seat. The two were in constant communication through an "open" mike on the intercom system.

When he started the jet engines, the roar drowned out attempted conversation because the cockpit canopies were kept open to allow cool air to flow over the occupants. When he taxied out the north-south runway, Davis closed the canopies and said: "We'll put it in afterburner on takeoff and go up to 10,000 feet in a maximum climb." This turned out to be straight up over Layton Avenue on the north side of the airport.

Clear of other traffic, he put the plane through aerobatic maneuvers over Lake Michigan, first rolling it around slowly and then doing two fast rolls one after another. The ride was so smooth that it seemed like the earth rather than the airplane had spun around.

"I'll show you what negative G's are like," Davis said . . . and pulled the plane's nose up in what appeared to be the start of an outside loop.

At the top of the loop, as the nose went gently down, weightlessness occurred. His passenger, who thought he was tightly strapped down into the seat, found himself actually lifted upward out of the seat.

A notebook on my lap, which also became weightless, floated up and away.

"This is exactly how the astronauts feel," Davis said. "I wouldn't want to do this for a long period of time."

As the plane headed downward, weight came back, and the notebook dropped on the floor of the cockpit . . ..

After doing a loop and flying upside down for a time, Davis put the nose down steeply, and the plane sped toward the ground. At only a few thousand feet altitude and 10 miles west of the airport, he called the tower and asked for permission to buzz the field.

Permission was granted, and the controller told aircraft on the ground awaiting takeoff clearance to watch to the southwest for the show.

The Phantom, at treetop, sped over the ground so fast that it appeared to Davis that he did not stay around long enough to be seen by an audience, the other participants at the air show.

"Tower this is Angel 7. How about my coming around again?" Again permission came without hesitation.

Davis came around and seemed to be even lower than on the first pass, if this was possible.

As he pulled up in a left turn, the tower controller asked in envy: "Need any help to drive that plane?"

"We get asked that a lot," Davis said over the intercom. "The Phantom never fails to impress people."

Davis's PR flights numbered many, if one considers the shows and stops at air fields the Blues made during the years in which Harley commanded the team. The tradition and practice of the PR man, Pilot No. 7, to take folks on rides continues today.

[1] Blue Angels 1970 U.S. Flight Demonstration Team.
[2] Newspaper articles, anecdotes, and narratives were taken from scrapbooks of J.D. Davis and other Blue Angels team members.

Chapter 9
POW Camp

The days of dazzling audiences, beach-side briefings before a show, thousands of people applauding a performance, and lazy days at "The Ranch" must have seemed to be nothing more than a dream or a distant memory as Hall wrapped his mind around his current situation after his shootdown over enemy territory.

The reality of Hall's condition could not have been more of a contrast from what he ever had undergone before. If during those first few days Hall was able to take a bath, the rare opportunity arrived only by special dispensation. The body lice, mosquitoes, and even the scorpions on the walls did not produce nearly the misery that simply being filthy did. A prisoner's hands become black paws with torn and ragged fingernails. He could try to forget whatever he knew about bacteria and health, sanitation and cleanliness. The inevitable, everpresent filth in a North Vietnamese prison camp covered floors, walls, food bowls—everything, everyone. The POW's just lived with the diarrhea. Was Hall in such a place?

The likely scenario appears to be that Hall was taken to a camp somewhere in Northern Vietnam, but here the mystery begins. Exactly where did Hall go? He seemed to disappear. If he survived the crash, if he were captured, if he were kept alive by the villagers he had been bombing for months, *and* if he were handed to the army, then his odds of being returned to U.S. forces were good, because the war was over; therefore, he soon would be set free. In camp he might have seen other

POW's and heard what happened to them. Would the captors torture Hall just days before his release? If they did, what would they expect to learn? Of what necessity would torturing Hall be, now that the war was over?

We know what happened to other POW's before Hall was captured. Soon after that first group of prisoners was released, stories appeared in *Time* and *Newsweek* about the extreme abuse and torture Americans had undergone in Vietnamese prisons. These stories that Mary Lou read dispelled her notion of humane treatment for the POW/MIA's.

In 1973 a *Time* article gave detailed information from newly released prisoners about the physical and mental torture they experienced. Navy CDR Richard Stratton said, "I have been tortured, beaten, put in solitary confinement, harassed, and humiliated."

"Air Force Capt. Joseph Mulligan said he treated and cured a badly burned arm by letting the maggots eat away the pus, then cleaning off the maggots with his own urine."[1]

Mary Lou learned that the favorite torture means of the North Vietnamese captors were lengths of rope, iron manacles, and fan belts. Prisoners stated that for interminable periods of time they were tied up into positions that devotees of yoga could not assume. Ropes tied to a man's ankles, wrists, and neck were tightened until he was bent backward into a donut shape. Men also were bent forward into a position of a baby sucking its toe. The ropes cut off circulation. In several cases for months and even years afterward the ropes left the victims with paralyzed limbs. As she read these graphic articles, Mary Lou felt as if she were there herself.

To be held in solitary confinement was not uncommon for many U.S. senior officers. CAPT James Mulligan was kept alone for three-and-a-half years. Col. Robinson Risner was isolated for four-and-a-half years. Where did they put Hall?

Mulligan related his experiences: "You are kept isolated in a small cell with no sound and no fresh air. I was kept like an animal in a solid cage, worse than an animal. I could not even see out. I did not see the moon for four-and-a-half years."

Most prisoners only received two meals a day; the meals were six hours apart. That food might consist of nothing more than a bowl of watery soup that occasionally had a fish head in it. The bread usually was wormy; the rice had sand mixed through it. LCDR Knutson said that he ate with one hand on his rice and the other on his soup bowl to keep the cockroaches from taking control.[2]

For these POW's much of the torture was intended to force confessions or to extract information. Often prisoners were beaten unconscious to force them to sign statements about the humanity of their treatment!

Another story Mary Lou read in *Time* was about Air Force Ace Maj. James Kasler, one of the legendary figures of the Vietnam War. A *Time* correspondent in Saigon interviewed Kasler just after his 72nd mission. On his 73rd mission he was shot down and captured. *Time* interviewed him again after he was released from the POW camp.

"My right thigh was broken and a piece of bone eight-inches long had split off and jammed into my groin," he said. He landed some 50 miles south of Hanoi. About 15 villagers jumped him and tore off all his clothes except his shorts and then wrapped him in a fishing net and hid him while planes circled overhead trying to find him. Once the planes finally left, they lashed him to a board, put him in the back of a pickup, and drove him north. When they reached Han Lo Prison (the "Hanoi Hilton"), guards began to beat him. "I could not believe that they would beat an injured prisoner, but I found out later that was their technique to break you. You were most vulnerable when first captured and injured. I finally wrote something like, 'We should seek peace at the peace table.' My reward was a shot of penicillin."

When he reached Hanoi, Kasler's right thigh-bone had been set with a clamp, but his leg continued to swell under a full body cast. The cast finally was removed and the leg lanced, but then the leg puffed up to twice its normal size. For most of the first winter he lay in a fever; he alternately was freezing and roasting. His roommate, Air Force Capt. John Brodak, during 40-degree nights gave up his own blanket to keep Kasler warm. "I'm probably here because of his care," Kasler acknowledged.

By mid-August 1966 the torturing of prisoners began in earnest. The Vietnamese had discovered that the prisoners were communicating with each other by tapping on the concrete walls. They wanted to punish the guilty. Kasler certainly was punished. Using the prisoner's special code Kasler could send a message through five rooms and receive an answer in 10 minutes. "We really got good at it . . .. The price for being caught was high." They [the guilty] were put into manacles that screwed down to the bone. Then they were tied with ropes that cut off the blood supply to their arms. Many of the men had wrists broken and arms dislocated. After 45 minutes of unspeakable anguish the beatings began. Ears were slapped until the eardrums bled. The torture could go on for days. Fan belts and rubber hoses could make a man confess to anything. And they did. The prisoners were kicked and punched. In Kasler's case the iron pin inserted into his right leg to stabilize his thigh bone was broken loose and jammed three-quarters of an inch into his hip bone. Kasler reports that many others were tortured until they died.[3]

Reading these stories made Mary Lou sick. *Why couldn't the military do something?* But she could do nothing for Harley. All she could do was keep reading.

In March 1973 *Newsweek* published an article about Douglas Ramsay, a young Foreign Service Agent working with the Agency for International Development. The Viet Cong mistook him for a CIA operative and marched him into a remote prison camp in Tay Ninh Province. At night they used leg irons to shackle him to trees. Douglas spent six of the next seven years in solitary confinement. In 1966 for 60 hours he was in a coma caused by cerebral malaria. "When I awoke, I found that every single superficial blood vessel in my head, arms, and legs had swollen shut." Ramsay was saved only because a prison doctor arrived literally within 60 seconds of his going into convulsions.

Ramsay said, "Even in the best of times, daily life was a nightmare of bamboo cages, boils, and a stomach-turning diet relieved only by an occasional chunk of dog or monkey meat, with bear meat as a laxative. We ate man's best friend and man's closest relative on a number of occasions, and liked it."

The POW's had little choice. Ramsay developed a lifesaving ability to overcome nausea and fend off starvation, He consumed his own vomit. The Viet Cong did attempt to maintain the fiction that the prisoners were receiving the same food the prison guards ate, but clearly that never was true. Ramsay watched in fury as the VC guards tossed peanuts to the chickens at a time when the POW's could have avoided the worst ravages of beri-beri with the vitamin of B1 found in the nuts. Ramsay emerged from the jungle in the first group of POW's to return home.[4]

But exactly what happened to Hall?

[1]"POW's: At Last the Story Can Be Told."
[2]Ibid.
[3]"Beyond the Worst Suspicions."
[4]"Bamboo Cages, Boils, and Six Years in Solitary."

Chapter 10
The War at Home

One March morning Mary Lou awoke with a start. She realized her baby was due in only two weeks! She had no nursery ready. In the corner of Mary Lou's bedroom she and Robin Davis, who had been living with Mary Lou since Hall's plane went down, busily began putting together some baby furnishings.

Just a bit thereafter a second jolt hit Mary Lou. The mail arrived. Harley had been missing for a few weeks. Mary Lou, however, still had not recovered from the shock of his being shot down. A letter with Harley's writing on the envelope was included in that day's mail! The letter had been posted from the *USS Enterprise* just before Harley's last flight.

26 January 1973
Gulf of Tonkin
Letter #60

My most precious Mary Lou,
    I received your letters #12 and #14 yesterday. Hon, I need to be told, just as you do, about your satisfaction with your partner for life, me. I respect you for the woman you are and just can't tell you what it means to me when you tell me how happy you are in your marriage, despite the bad deals that go along with it. I am probably more aware of your feeling about the cruises than you might think and the fact that you tolerate them

does a lot to ease my mind. I'm constantly involved with the decisions about emergency leave for the men and they all stem from the wife not being able to hack the separation. I use you for my standard in dealing with a lot of these problems.

From watching my dad get trapped for life in a job that he never enjoyed, I just have always thought that when the end of your life comes, you can't look back on what might have been if . . . . I love you with so much depth and feelings and always pray that you understand my decisions about my life and general philosophy. I would give up everything for you without hesitation. The fact that you never asked, even though I know there are times when you would like to, is a continual source of deep pride and appreciation. The Navy isn't the life and career for everyone and perhaps if I had met you earlier, I wouldn't be here today. But on the other hand, a man must be able to live with himself, and for me that is doing the best job possible in what you have chosen and committed to do. It does hurt me to be out here and have you and Heather so far away, but deep inside I know that you are raising my children as I would want them raised and I pray that Heather will be able to understand what her old man is doing, when she is old enough. Without your love and understanding she could never have the chance.

Have been so busy you can't believe. We flew 29 sorties today. As a result, here I sit jotting off a quick letter. We have a big day tomorrow, then no one knows what will really happen. We are drawing very little ground fire that we see anyway and so we feel that the risk is minimal. Both sides are really trying to pour it on the final days. It is 1:00 a.m. and I must close now and

get some sleep.
I love you.
Harley

Again Mary Lou felt devastation wash over her. It enveloped her and crushed her. The emotions, the reality, the surreal experience—all left her saddened and unsettled. As grateful as she was for the letter and for her seeing Harley's handwriting, reading his words to her, and recognizing his love for her reopened every single wound. The words appeared as if Harley from his prison cell had called out to her, "*I love you!*" The rest of the morning she cried.

As if the morning's events weren't sufficiently upsetting, later that day as she returned with baby supplies from the Commissary, Mary Lou found Bruce Bailey, her CACO, sitting on her steps waiting for her.

"I have some wonderful news," he said. "CDR Hall's status has been changed from Missing In Action to Prisoner Of War."

"Why? What has happened?"

"Based on the facts," Bruce said.

"What facts?"

"Based on the facts that there were two good parachutes and that LT Terry Heath said he saw him running on the ground."

"But we have known that all along. What is different?"

"I don't know if there is anything else or what the Navy knows that we don't. They just changed his status based on the known facts. CDR Hall is now officially a Prisoner of War."

Mary Lou did not care what they called Harley. She just wanted him home. After Bailey's visit she started receiving information through the back channels—informal confidences between friends. Her friend Bill Switzer spoke with a debriefer he knew at Balboa Hospital. Switzer, in turn, repeated to Mary

Lou what the debriefer had told him: "I am betraying a trust, but I have to tell you this. We have not talked before, but I know how close you were to CDR Hall, and I know how this has affected you. I just want to tell you—do not worry. He is there. They have him. He is coming back."

The first group of POW's were returned February 12, 1973. Harley was not among them. Switzer again spoke with his debriefer friend; once more the man told Switzer not to worry . . . that Harley would be home. The second group of planes in Operation Homecoming, the name for the 1973 operation which brought POW's out of Vietnam, saw even more Americans return. Harley still was not among the returning POW's. Again Switzer talked with his friend. This time the friend told Switzer he could not tell him anything else. The third group of repatriates was to be released soon. Everyone expected Hall to be on the final plane out of Vietnam.

Then Mary Lou had a call from Dr. Roger Shields, Deputy Assistant Secretary of Defense, who said, "I did not call sooner because I wanted to wait until I had some information that was accurate. Your husband's case is one of the most compelling I have seen. They are holding your husband, Mrs. Hall. One way or the other, they will have to answer for this. Never settle for anything else."

Robin was at the Commissary at Miramar when she saw a former POW, a man whom she knew. He had returned from Vietnam in the first group. She asked him about Hall. He reported bluntly and frankly to Robin, "Yes, they have him. Don't worry. He will be home."

Mary Lou was home alone when the third group of Operation Homecoming aircraft carrying POW's landed at Clark Air Force Base, Republic of the Philippines. On television she watched as the POW's exited the plane, walked down those long stairs, and were saluted as soon as their feet touched the pavement. Although almost all were able to walk, some of the men looked very badly treated. For years some had been held as prisoners—the longest for eight-and-a-half years. Holding her breath Mary Lou watched for each new face and scrutinized each man's features as he appeared in the doorway. Then out walked Al Kientzler! Al was Hall's backseater—his RIO! Because of the leg wound he suffered after the shootdown, Kientzler walked slowly as he used crutches. Mary Lou *knew* Harley was going to be next out of that door!

But the next person was not Harley, nor was the next nor the next. The planes, emptied of their precious passengers, sat abandoned on the tarmac. The focus of everyone else turned toward the joyful scene of greeting the men. *Empty!* Mary Lou didn't know what to do. *This can't be! This has to be a mistake! Harley has to be in the plane! Where is Harley?* Tears rolled down her cheeks. She felt a panic overtaking her. Mary Lou flipped stations and hoped for another look at the prisoners descending the stairs so that she could see their faces one more time. *Harley had to be there!* Some horrid mistake had happened!

For days afterward she cried. *What had happened to Harley? The cease-fire had long ago happened. Other planeloads of the POW's had arrived. What was he doing still in Vietnam? Why didn't he return? Where is he? Who is with Harley?*

The panic, the fear, the desperate need for news of Harley and her impending delivery of a second baby produced incredible pressure on Mary Lou. On the following Tuesday she saw her obstetrician, Dr. Jones. He decided if she didn't go into labor by Thursday, he would induce labor. To her every day seemed 40-hours long. She couldn't stop crying. Every breathing moment of her life was stretched between the baby *in utero*, rambunctious 4-year-old Heather, and Harley, her precious husband being held prisoner in Vietnam.

On Thursday, after Robin took Heather to the sitter, she drove Mary Lou to the hospital. Mary Lou checked into the hospital. Dr. Jones stopped by to examine her. He asked whether Mary Lou were ready to deliver her baby.

"Oh, I'm plenty ready."

"That baby just doesn't want to be born, does it? Well, you just relax. We'll let the medication take effect. I am going to get a bite to eat, but I will be back soon." He smiled reassuringly. "The baby will be here soon."

Actually the delivery began a little sooner than he anticipated. Mere minutes after he left the room, Mary Lou said to the nurse, "My bed is wet."

"You are just imagining, dear. The doctor times these things pretty well."

"No! I mean the bed is WET! I am not lying here imagining things. I know *wet*! The. Bed. Is. Wet!"

Just to reassure Mary Lou, the nurse, practised in consoling anxious moms-to-be, smiled and checked under the sheet. Then she yelled, "Oh, my!", and ran out of the room.

Mary Lou thought, *What on earth is happening?*

Robin was out in the fathers' waiting room and was making Christmas ornaments—months in advance of Christmas. She made Christmas ornaments all year long. She had gathered up every ashtray in the room, cleaned them, and filled them with beads and pins. When the flock of nurses ran past the waiting room, Robin, along with the fathers, looked up and wondered where the nurses were going.

Mary Lou's room suddenly was full of nurses. She was losing consciousness, being slapped, and given oxygen. She kept asking, "What on earth?" Once again she felt as if everything was collapsing in on her. Things in her life already had gone from bad to worse; now this complication was occurring in her baby's delivery! Mary Lou was breathing deeply. She was trying to do what the nurses told her to do but wondered whether now she were going to lose her baby.

Finally Dr. Jones was found. He returned to the room, lifted up the sheet, and said, "Quick! Get her to surgery!"

Placenta previa had occurred. Mary Lou was hemorrhaging. Jones reassured her that the baby was fine. Although people around her were panicking, when Jones told her he would have to perform a C-section, Mary Lou became the calmest person in the room.

"How big is the scar going to be?"

"Don't worry. I'll do a bikini cut."

Just as Jones had promised Mary Lou, the baby indeed was fine. She named the healthy baby boy Harley Stephen after his father and grandfather.

All the hospital staff and employees knew Mary Lou's situation. The nurses paid extra-close attention to her because her husband was a POW. During the week of her stay she had many visitors. At the time Mary Lou was going into surgery for the delivery, Bruce, her Casualty Assistance Officer, had dropped by the hospital, but Jones turned him away. Jones bluntly told him that Mary Lou was coping with all she could deal with and did not need any additional news, whether the news were good or bad.

That Dr. Jones asked Bruce to wait and that Bruce heeded that request proved wise. When Bruce did finally see Mary Lou, she was propped up in bed but still exhausted. His news was bad. Al Kientzler had been debriefed. He reported that he never once saw Hall after he landed—not in the field and not later in the POW camp. The Vietnamese captors had told Kientzler that Hall had been killed.

Mary Lou did not believe the report Bruce brought from Al's debriefer. She had heard from too many other credible sources that Harley was alive. Whether Al saw him or not did not prove otherwise. She knew Harley had survived.

Mary Lou was in a fragile physical and emotional condition. After Bruce's visit, as she lay in the hospital bed, she had time to think about her life—her situation. She was grateful for having the room to herself. She had asked the nurse not to assign anyone else to the room, because the sight of husbands celebrating with their wives the births of their new children would be too depressing. She didn't think she could withstand that. For many hours Mary Lou lay there as she tried to hold things together in her life. All week long the nurses kept her room empty. Finally on her very last night every other bed was filled. The staff had no choice but to put another new mother in her room. Mary Lou said watching those scenes of two parents rejoicing in the birth of their baby made that night the most difficult of all.

By the time Mary Lou arrived home from the hospital, the *USS Enterprise* had returned to home port. Because Robin's husband, J.D., now was home, Robin left Mary Lou's house to return to her own home. That left Mary Lou alone with the baby and Heather. Not long after the *Enterprise* docked, white-uniformed sailors delivered Hall's personal locker to her. In it she found Harley's clothes, the letters she had written him, pictures of her and Heather, and the small, portable typewriter he used to write letters to her. She had small parts of Harley, but she did not have Harley. How she wanted Harley home with her, baby Harley Stephen, and Heather! She had her family. She had her friends. She had her two precious children. She had her faith. But she didn't have Harley!

Chapter 11
Prisoner

After 27 years of fighting first the French and then the Americans the Viet Cong had developed a protocol for dealing with prisoners. If one so unlucky to be taken prisoner lived past the first hour, was not beaten to death, or was not shot, then he would be handed over to the regular North Vietnamese Army, who shackled the prisoner and assigned guards. When the army unit returned from the field, the soldiers in turn handed the prisoner to an officer with jurisdiction. This scenario occurred only *if* the captured American lived through the first hour. Many did not. The North Vietnamese people's hatred of American pilots was intense, hardened, and vicious. Flying so high in the clouds and dropping such devastation on the ground, the pilots were viewed as gods and therefore were beyond retribution. Many Vietnamese peasants believed that pilots could see 20,000 or 30,000 feet down to the ground. When an American pilot fell to the ground, old women and farmers were known to attack with pitchforks and knives. An individual Viet Cong soldier might only lay his hands on an American pilot once in his lifetime but would have years of grudges to settle. Many pilots were killed by the first Vietnamese to spot them. These acts were the primary concern of any pilot hitting that muddy ground. The experience of most downed pilots was to spend anywhere from hours to days in the field with their captors until the prisoners were relinquished to a camp commander elsewhere. Many were marched for kilometers or thrown into a truck. One can be absolutely certain that for all downed pilots, the first evening was a nightmare.

An F-4 pilot's fully packed survival vest contained an emergency pack which held a compass, a map, a knife, food rations, a beeper, a radio, and a .38 pistol. If he were not shot to pieces before he hit the ground and if he could, in fact, run and hide, he could activate his locator beeper and hopefully be rescued quickly.

Hall and Kientzler landed half a mile apart, so they were out of sight of each other on the ground. Hall, alone, knew well the evasive procedures to follow to avoid capture. When LT Terry Heath saw Hall running for cover, Hall had released his chute and left it blowing in the opposite direction from which he ran.

What could be known at that point was that Harley was alive and surely was feeling as scared and rattled as he ever had been in his life. He had heard the stories. He knew his life wasn't worth dirt until he was out of the field and handed over as a prisoner. Any single one of the 17-year-old-or-younger kid soldiers around him—kids who for months had been killing and living in the jungle—on a whim could shoot him. Only because of later events do we know Harley was not killed.

Cut off as few people ever are, Harley was the despised prisoner of war—unable to speak the language, unused to the food, if he had any food at all. Perhaps injured severely from beatings, he would not be given proper care. Abandonment appears in many forms, but the physical and emotional isolation Harley felt had to be immense. Sleeping naked on the ground, enduring the insects and the heat, manacled, abused in a language he did not speak . . . . How alone can a person be?

Harley would have had only certain solid bits of knowledge on which to hang. He knew the war was over. Prisoners already were being returned. He knew that sooner or later the U.S. Navy would rescue him and bring him home. He knew that before his release, he would be interrogated and maybe tortured. He knew that if he survived the next few days and was put into the prisoner system, eventually he would be Stateside. These things he knew.

Robinson Risner reported that when he was captured and taken prisoner, he was treated fairly well by the villagers—protected even—despite the fact he was stripped and marched for miles on a bad leg and bleeding feet. His capture happened, however, early in the war. He reports thinking fervently about his family, about their house and its rooms and furniture, and about his dear wife and children.[1] Most likely Harley's thoughts were the same—half a mind for what he was denied and half a mind for what might happen next.

A frantic time for the North Vietnamese, that January day on which Hall was shot down was the first day of the cease-fire. Their troops were rushing south to occupy South Vietnam. As a prisoner Hall would have to be moved north where the POW camps were, but who was going north? All the convoys and endless lines of trucks moving ant-like were headed south toward Saigon. *What to do with a captured American pilot? Hold onto him there? Take him south with the army? Try to send him with a detachment traveling north?* As a prisoner who happened to be a pilot, Hall would be the center of attention. Risner reported that the sight of an American pilot drew large, often hostile, crowds.[2] During this time was Harley injured and perhaps kept in a nearby village so that the injuries might heal?

The day of capture usually is so mind-numbing and overwhelming that only the next morning does reality really crash in. Wherever Hall awoke that next morning, he surely awoke with a start, a sigh, and a quick look around him. Tied up and sleeping on the ground or in a hut with a guard at the door, he would have awakened quickly and realized he still was exhausted. When he went to relieve himself, a guard likely stayed with him.

    They tortured him. They did so as surely as they followed every other portion of their routine. Elbows tied together behind his back. Arms or legs broken. Hanged from the ceiling with dislocated shoulders. Psychological torture. "You are never going home. Your country has abandoned you. You will never see your family again." The abuse could have started that first day or the day after. Abuse did happen. No question: Harley would have been in living hell!

    [1] "POW's: At Last the Story Can Be Told."
    [2] Ibid.

Chapter 12
Hall Alone

After six months of captivity what was Hall thinking? Probably that something had gone terribly wrong. If he were not in isolation, then was he surrounded by jubilant Vietnamese who declared their victory in every way possible? Did they treat Hall worse? Was he the captured foe who truly had no recourse? With other prisoners the possibility of eventual release created complications for the North Vietnamese government. By the end of the war—the time Hall was shot down—the North Vietnamese had learned their lesson. For the North Vietnamese, admitting the existence of a prisoner wanted for interrogation started the clock on his eventual release. To maintain total control of a prisoner the Viet Cong first must declare him dead. Severing any ongoing concern about a prisoner simply made sense only if they wanted to keep him long-term.

To his captors CDR Hall seemed a last-minute prize. If his notoriety as a former Commander of the Blue Angels worked for the North Vietnamese and against Hall, his familiarity with tactical planning made him even more valuable to Communist leaders. Perhaps the Chinese or Soviets wanted to interrogate him. Or maybe someone in command just wanted a trophy to keep as a final dig at the Americans.

Pure vengeance plays a part. As a motive for Hall's indefinite imprisonment, revenge cannot be ignored. If for many, many years a person hates someone deeply enough, the opportunity to exact a bit of cruelty at the end may be irresistible. Communist North Vietnam had reasons we can surmise, and probably others we can't, for keeping CDR Hall. All we know for sure is that they kept him. But what of Hall? Six months of physical torture would have broken his body—if that's what the captors wanted to do to him. But the psychological torture would have been even worse than the physical. CDR Hall did not have the one tiny advantage other POW's in North Vietnam had: as long as the war was being prosecuted, the POW's were warehoused and expected to be part of a final treaty. The end of the war, if they survived, meant the end of their imprisonment. Once the war was over and the treaty signed, however, what could a prisoner expect for himself and his future were he left behind in captivity? What could he expect in the way of mercy from his captors?

After a certain point, months and months after his capture, Hall probably did not expect much. His future had shrunk to a pinpoint. Nothing but staying alive was ahead for him—and only if he could manage that. The North Vietnamese likely told him, and he likely believed, that the world thought he was dead. After months have passed, what happens to the mind of a man who is imprisoned for what he thinks will be a few weeks? Six months, nine months after his capture, Harley could have been wild with despair. In whatever hole or hut or cell or cage they had him chained, whether in a city or in the jungle, he was as alone as a man can be. That aloneness we can conclude as fact.

Epictetus, the Greek philosopher and slave, said that "even the most abject slave still controls his own fate as long as he chooses to remain alive." At some point Hall, abject and perhaps despairing, looked down this dark hole. Maybe he waited a year or two or three, but he surely looked; yet, we know that 15 years later when he was interrogated by the Soviets, he was alive. He looked in, but he did not fall down the hole.

Chapter 13
Down in Flames

For the Blue Angels, bad luck was everywhere in 1973, the year after Hall rotated off the team and returned to Vietnam. LCDR Don Bentley became the new Blue Angels Leader. First, Hall was shot down and captured; he became the only Blue Angels Leader ever captured. Secondly, the Blues were practicing maneuvers during Winter Training in El Centro, CA. Something went horribly wrong. Three of the planes in the Diamond formation collided in mid-air. Although all the pilots ejected safely, Bentley injured his back. He was unable to continue his tour on the team. Another leader had to be selected.

LCDR Skip Umstead was stationed at Miramar in San Diego when the call arrived from the Navy admiral in charge of the Blue Angels. "LCDR Umstead, we want you to be the new Blue Angels Leader. Are you interested?"

"Yes, Sir!" Umstead answered. Like every other fighter pilot in the Navy, he wanted to be leader of the Blue Angels. Umstead, for two years a member of CDR Hall's team, actually stayed a third year with the Blues because the two-year rotation was off-schedule. Umstead assumed command of the Blues and led the team on a European tour that included performances at the Paris International Air Show, Spain, Turkey, Iran, and Italy.

On July 23, 1973, the Blues traveled from NAS Pensacola to Naval Air Engineering Station Lakehurst, in Lakehurst, NJ. When the team traveled, the crew chiefs (aircraft engine mechanics) assigned to the specific F-4s flew the backseats of those planes. As the group neared the show site, if the planes contained adequate fuel, the pilots performed arrival maneuvers, a mini-demonstration. On this trip, to refuel, the group had stopped at NAS Oceana, near Virginia Beach, VA. The short distance to NAS Lakehurst gave them more than enough fuel to do their arrival performance. Because of hydraulic problems, however, plane No. 2 remained at NAS Oceana. Plane No. 4 moved into No. 2's right-wing spot in the Diamond. The Diamond was formed with three-aircraft rather than the usual four. As was customary the Blues began the opening formation, a Diamond Loop. They were flying in very low, thick clouds in windy conditions. As their planes went to the top of the loop and started back down on the back side of the loop, Murphy's plane struck Umstead's. Umstead's backseater, Petty Officer First Class Gerald Harve (POIC), ejected and parachuted to safety. Umstead, Murphy, and Murphy's backseater, POIC Ronald Thomas, however, were killed.

Mary Lou was home watching the news on television when the reporter announced the Blue Angels crash. Her phone immediately rang; the Commanding Officer at El Centro called and told her that two Blue Angels and one backseater had died. These men she knew personally; they were three men for whom she cared deeply. Umstead had flown with Harley. The news seemed incredible. According to the Commander and the news report no one yet had a clue how the accident had occurred or what had gone wrong. Mike Murphy's girlfriend already had called to ask Mary Lou for information. Ernie Christensen, who by then was at Mary Lou's, took the call and reluctantly told Mike's girlfriend that Mike had not survived.[1]

LCDR J.D. Davis was able to secure a military plane to fly the Blue Angels and their family members from Miramar to the funeral at Pensacola. Mary Lou was allowed to fly on the plane with the group because her husband was listed as a POW and still was considered a member of the military.

The flight was somber and quiet. Mary Lou sat alone and grieved for the families of the three fliers. She thought long on the vicissitudes of life—how events can overcome a person and radically change everything he or she knows. Nearly every minute of the day she thought about Harley. He was alive some place—a place from which no one seemed to be able to reach him nor save him. Much of the time she wondered what he was doing *right that moment*. That he might be dead was inconceivable. But she had to be realistic. She had to think about Heather and little Harley. She had to be strong for them so that this misery would not destroy their lives as well.

Mary Lou, however, never had faced a challenge so overwhelming. She definitely was having trouble adjusting. Her life had changed so fast. Only a short time ago she, Harley, and Heather had been together on the beach in Pensacola; they had spent a wonderful day there. Harley helped Heather build a sand castle while Mary Lou lay on a beach towel. She remembered the sugar-white sand at Destin Beach near Pensacola, the afternoon sun on the water, and the breeze that blew over them. After Harley finished building the sand castle with Heather, he lay down beside Mary Lou. They soon were joined by Heather with her small bucket and shovel. Mary Lou and Harley talked quietly together as Heather attempted to fill her bucket with sand. She slung half of it on the towel and on Harley and Mary Lou.

After Heather had half-buried them with sand, they all swam and played in the waves. Mary Lou was bobbing Heather in her bright orange life jacket in the waves while Harley floated on their raft. Heather laughed and tried jumping into the waves; she soon wore herself out.

That day Harley was in high spirits. Even though Heather was starting to tire, he didn't want to lose this family time.

"Girls, let's take a walk to find sea shells!" Heather perked right back up. They walked and gathered some shells until Heather was too tired; then to wash off the sand they headed to the showers on the boardwalk.

In their sandals and cover-ups over their swimsuits, they walked into the beachfront restaurant, one of their favorite eating spots. As they ate their appetizers, the big ceiling fans turned slowly. Their wet suits and bodies dried. Another patron stopped at their table to ask Harley for his autograph and remarked enthusiastically, "I just love the Blue Angels shows! We always go!"

"Sure," Harley said. His smile was a mile wide. In every way the day was a perfect day. As the three of them sat there and looked out at the crystal-clear blue water and white, sugar sand, an occasional deep-sea fishing boat or shrimp boat went by.

"Gosh, I am going to miss Pensacola," Harley said. "I just hope our next assignment is somewhere as great as this."

Bringing Mary Lou back to the present, the plane shook slightly as it began its descent. She began to cry. Harley, the other three pilots—everything seemed so tremendously unfair. She turned her head to the side so the others on the aircraft could not see her. She felt no resolve for the future or anything else. Her world still seemed to be crashing around her. When they landed, out her window Mary Lou saw the Blue Angels hangar and knew she wasn't going to be able to control the tears. Only six months had passed since her loss of Harley.

She jumped up by saying, "Ladies first," and headed up the aisle. She exited the plane before anyone else. Robin was waiting for her at the bottom of the stairs. She took one look at Mary Lou and knew Mary Lou was about to lose the last vestige of her self-control. Robin grabbed her, "Let's go to the bathroom." The two of them stayed there while Mary Lou cried and cried until finally she was all cried out. Once she was composed and had repaired her makeup, Mary Lou was better able to face the group.

The Barrancas National Cemetery, NAS Pensacola was filled with thousands of military white marble headstones in perfect rows—all 42-inches long, 13-inches wide, and four-inches thick with slightly rounded tops. Mary Lou looked out over the many graves around her. As Mary Lou stood with other Blue Angels and family members under two large, green oak trees, time seemed to stand still; the atmosphere was quiet and calming. Mary Lou and Robin stood with Harley's teammates and their wives. Present were Jim Maslowski, Mary and Kevin O'Mara, Bill Switzer, Susan and Jack Keen, Ernie Christensen, J.D. Davis, and others. All talked quietly. An all-surrounding sense of oneness prevailed. They were burying LCDR Skip Umstead.

The Naval Officer who was conducting the ceremony stepped to the graveside and began:

> The Blue Angels creed says, "The prestige of wearing the Blue Angel uniform carries with it an extraordinary honor, one that reflects not only on you as an individual but on your teammates and the entire squadron." His teammates respected Skip and held him in high regard. He wore the uniform with dignity and honor. The creed also reads, "Once a Blue Angel, always a Blue Angel."

Navy sailors stood straight and tall by the chapel and shot their guns into the air in a 21-gun salute to honor Skip. Just as the salute ended, above the chapel the Air Force Thunderbirds flew low and loud with red-and-blue vapor trailing from the wingtips of their planes. They flew the Delta formation minus one—the Missing Man formation, the most impressive aerial salute many people had ever seen. Chill bumps stood on arms. Tears streamed down cheeks. Mary Lou felt her grief was bottomless. For her this brief service felt almost as if it were Harley's funeral.

Mary Lou walked over to speak with Skip's parents. She told them how much Harley admired Skip and Skip's abilities as a pilot.

"I wanted to bury Skip here at Pensacola," his mother said, "where he was the happiest he has ever been. Being a Blue Angel was the greatest thing that ever happened to him and the thing he loved most."

"You are right," Mary Lou said. She appreciated the wisdom of the older woman. "Being a Blue Angel is a rare and privileged life. Most people never get the chance."

She left the funeral aware of the very privileged life she and Harley had together. That seemed to balance the scale of things a little. She had a better sense of the future and was perking up when a woman she didn't know remarked, "Everything these guys do as a Blue Angel is larger than life. Even their funeral is larger than life."

Mary Lou looked at the woman with a resolve she had not felt in a long time. *Yes, you are right,* she thought, *a privileged life*. Harley and she had a rare and precious relationship. They had taken advantage of their time together. Harley loved their time together as much as she did. He developed a passion for golf and played when he and Steve, Mary Lou's father, were together. But he never accepted other invitations for golf. One day he explained why. Playing golf took him from his family for one whole day. He wanted to be with Mary Lou and Heather. But he really liked golf. Solution: He told Mary Lou they would go to the golf course; she would take lessons. She did. Mary Lou learned to play golf! That was fine with her.

A few days after that horrid night Mary Lou had learned of Harley's shootdown, she and her mother took a walk to visit Pam Switzer. As they walked, Mary Lou tried to describe this special somethingness she and Harley shared. Throughout their marriage she knew what could happen to Harley because of the dangers involved in his career. She didn't want to look back and have regrets about their life together. She didn't. She was happy. She remembered times she and Harley were in church. When the minister said, "Let's pray together," she didn't need to ask God for anything other than protection for Harley. She had Harley. She had Heather. She had everything she needed and needed nothing else. She was happy.

She was glad she had attended the funeral. Attending the service had given her a new perspective on events. Grieving with others also had given unity to what she had been experiencing alone. She had a lot to live up to. Mary Lou had high standards for herself, just as Harley had for himself. She remembered her words to him in Hong Kong, "Harley, we know it's almost over. Please don't go doing more than you need to do."

He always went above and beyond expectations. For Harley she would move on. She would begin the process of picking up the pieces of her life and carrying on.

After that horrifying accident the remainder of the 1973 show season schedule was canceled. The Secretary of the Navy was not in favor of keeping the Blue Angels Team. Shivers ran through past and present team members. The Blues embodied much tradition and history. To lose the Blue Angels, such a bright spot in Naval Aviation history, would be the unthinkable, a travesty—a shame. Blue Angels symbolize what is best about America and what Americans believe about themselves. They also personify diligent, thorough work and being the best one can be. Navy pilots dream about being a Blue Angel; that

121

dream was something the Navy could not afford to lose.

The Blue Angels did fly again. Admiral Zumwalt, Chief of Naval Operations, rescued them. He insisted that the Navy keep the Blue Angels Team, but the Secretary of the Navy agreed only with the stipulation that the team first be reformed as a command and secondly that the team change to a plane that was less difficult a show aircraft to fly and maintain as well as change to one more fuel efficient. In 1974 the A-4 Skyhawk became the new plane for the Blue Angels. With one engine instead of two the Skyhawk was not nearly as fast as the Phantom, but it had much more fuel efficiency. The lighter plane, however, was capable of most of the same maneuvers that aided the team in producing shows that were consistent with the historic "ballet in the sky" that was the mantra of the Blue Angels teams.

The show schedule resumed. Not one Blue Angel, however, forgot the losses of 1973.[2] No doubt the plight of the exceptional former commander of the Blues, Harley Hall, frequently sprang to mind.

[1]Interviews with Mary Lou Hall, Davis, Christensen.
[2]Herbert and Blue Angel Video.

Chapter 14
Left Alive

Released POW Frank Anton, in his book *Why Didn't You Get Me Out?: A POW's Nightmare in Vietnam*, avows his certainty that many POW and MIA's were left alive in Vietnam. He knew that hundreds of men who still were alive in Vietnam when POW's were released in 1973 and points to the fact that no POW's who were amputees or who had suffered the sort of massive trauma associated with ejecting from a jet aircraft were released. Nor were any prisoners released who had suffered serious burns common from missile hits. Anton declares he is 99-percent sure we left men in Vietnam; "[b]ut there was a real effort to silence POWs on the question of Americans left behind. The government denied any such thing had happened and made it clear to those in the military that their careers hung on 'toeing the line.'"[1] After Anton was home five months, he was asked to speak at a local community college in Ocean County, NJ, near his parents' home. The college planned a discussion of the Vietnam War. On stage Anton was joined by an Air Force colonel assigned to the Pentagon. A young man in the audience asked Anton, "Were there men left alive and abandoned in Vietnam?"

"'Sure! Absolutely! I know there were."

"But the audience saw the colonel become visibly agitated. As an official representative of the Pentagon, he could not let the statement stand. When he spoke, he tried to be diplomatic, 'Frank, I like you personally, but this is wrong of you to give these people false hope.'"

Anton responded with his own experiences. He had personally seen both a chopper pilot and a wounded B-52 pilot held in Laos; neither man returned in Operation Homecoming. For the public record, he gave the two men's names. The colonel dismissed Anton's remarks as if Anton were naïve and ill-informed. Speaking on behalf of the Pentagon the colonel assured the audience that the U.S. Government would never leave Americans behind. For many years hence this position would be the government's official one.

In the book Anton reports that a few weeks later another colonel at the Pentagon called him. "Look, we know we left people back there. We are doing everything we can to get them back, but your talking about it does not help a thing!"

Anton was not convinced. He continued to talk about the men remaining in Vietnam and gave interviews that spread the word that the Vietnam issue was far from closed. Anton averred that men still were waiting to be rescued from their prisons. Then he received a call from a brigadier general at the Pentagon. The man went straight to the point, "Do you want to stay in the military?" The Army official waited until he heard Anton's response and then said, "Stop talking about the POW issue." The military was Anton's life. Because he did not want to lose his career, he stopped talking. "I have been uncomfortable and ashamed of my decision ever since," Anton writes.

The U.S. government seemed to take the position that all POW's who were alive had been returned home, even though 5,000 prisoners were on the list and only 591 were released. Some people, however, did not readily accept this stance. Angered families who had missing relatives protested and started the National League of Families of American Prisoners and Missing in Action in Southeast Asia. In a van covered with a large sign that bore this message: "All POW/MIA's are NOT home!",[2] wives of MIA's drove around the White House. The government could not keep quiet the families who had relatives who were reportedly seen alive in Vietnam. Another problem for the government was that of returning POW and MIA's who told their stories to media across the nation.

Mary Lou and other wives constantly wrote letters to the government. The Episcopal priest from the church Harley and Mary Lou attended had introduced Mary Lou to the wife of another POW. She and Mary Lou shared similar circumstances: her husband had been shot down in 1972. In their POW/MIA situations he and Harley shared commonalities. His and Harley's careers had followed the same paths. She had three sons. Harley Stephen and her youngest son were very good friends. Two other wives became part of the group. The four women became very close friends. One of them lived only three houses from Mary Lou. They were smart women and knowledgeable about the military. Together they knew many, many people and whom to call. Relentlessly they asked questions and demanded answers. Mary Lou avers, "The government didn't know what to do with us! This is the first time the government had to deal with families not accepting blindly what they were told. They didn't know how to make us go away." Anything that concerned Harley, Mary Lou could not ignore or give up. Each response to the numerous letters she wrote indicated the government had no new information about Hall. Most government officials adopted the same line: they had no information about any POW's left alive in Vietnam or Laos.

Both Congress and President Nixon made moves to stop not only the war but also to complete the POW/MIA issue. The War Powers Resolution, passed by Congress on November 7, 1973, gave Congress the power to stop the use of U.S. Armed Forces that the President had ordered into combat in Vietnam or other parts of the world. This resolution, the strongest action ever taken by Congress, gave Congress war-making powers over the President. Nixon, therefore, could not send troops back to Vietnam without Congress's approval, which Congress never gave.[3] The War Powers Resolution placed the Democrat-controlled Congress in the middle of the POW situation. On January 2, 1973, before the cease fire, the House Democratic caucus voted by a margin of two to one in favor of cutting off all funds for military operations in Indochina, provided Hanoi allowed our forces to withdraw safely and all American POW's were released. Nixon privately had assured South Vietnam's President Thieu that U.S. troops would be back in South Vietnam if the North Vietnamese did not follow agreements of the cease-fire agreement. When all the POW's were not sent home, Nixon no longer controlled the troops. His decision was to let the issue die. He also was in the middle of the Watergate scandal. White House tapes recorded on March 27, 1973, and removed from Nixon's office revealed that in a discussion with his advisors about how to get out from underneath the horrific combination of the ongoing Vietnam nightmare and the looming Watergate crisis, Nixon said, "My view would be to get the Vietnam (issue) out of the way. . . ." Two days later, however, Nixon's speech to the nation contained this contradictory statement: "For the first time in 12 years, no American military forces are in Vietnam. All our American POW's are on their way home."[4]

Was Nixon's statement the same sentiment of others in the government and the public? Did Nixon and Congress signal the end of all hope for Harley and other POW's? Was all hope of Harley's existence eradicated? Surely someone would step forward to find the POW's left in Vietnam and to learn the fate of MIA's. What more could Mary Lou do?

[1]Anton 170-183.
[2]"MIA Families: Living Death".
[3]World Book.
[4]Nixon.

Chapter 15
Proof of Life

Message traffic on February 29, 1980, at NAS Miramar contained information about the official status of some POW's. An acquaintance of Mary Lou's friend Jean saw the message, recognized Jean's husband's name, and called her. In turn Jean called Mary Lou. Both of their husbands, as well as the husbands of their two friends, Carleen and Jan, had been declared dead! None of the women had received official notification— no visit, no telegram, no telephone call. Other POW's and MIA's long before had been declared dead. These men, their husbands, were the last four Navy POW's/MIA's to be declared dead. Mary Lou called her CACO, Bruce Bailey. At Miramar he found the message, verified its content, and spoke with Mary Lou.

The next day, March 1, 1980, late in the morning, all four wives received telegrams which notified them of the change to their husbands' statuses. (According to official military protocol, a personal notification was the official means to inform the next of kin of any change of status, whether injury, death, or reclassification.) Making no personal visit was a breech of U.S. Navy protocol.

Jean walked down to Mary Lou's. Carleen arrived shortly. When Jan entered Mary Lou's house, Jan was holding her telegram. She told them she didn't want to open it. Eventually the other three women persuaded her to open the envelope. When she did, she read the contents and began to laugh hysterically. Regaining control she related that two telegrams were inside the envelope—one addressed to a man being notified of an eviction, the other, permission for certain family members to spread over the Pacific the ashes of their deceased loved one. Later that morning Western Union delivered to Mary Lou's house Jan's correct telegram.

For Mary Lou the telegram didn't change a thing about Harley. The only change was in finances. During his POW/MIA status Hall had been promoted to Captain. Because he had served 23 years in the Navy, he was eligible for retirement. The Navy considered him retired. As his widow, Mary Lou would receive a monthly check for 55 percent of Hall's retirement benefit. The allotment was just enough money to cover her mortgage on the house with some left for food and utilities—in other words, barely enough money to live a modest, frugal life. With the exception of her financial situation, for Mary Lou nothing about Harley had changed. He still was gone. She still didn't know where he was. She still wanted him home with her and the children.

Mary Lou moved forward—rearing her children, writing letters. Years passed. Little or no news about the POW's appeared. The issue of missing Americans in Vietnam fell off the political agenda in Washington. Some congress members and Senators kept up the fight, but the subject of POW's and MIA's was not something people often saw on the news or on talk shows. For Americans life had gone on. But for Mary Lou and some thousands of others like her, men like her Harley truly never had been forgotten.

Amazingly, one day the unthinkable—the unlikely—happened! Proof of life occurred in a very unexpected way. In 1993 Mary Lou had another official visitor. He gave her information from the Defense Intelligence Agency (DIA) headquartered in Washington, DC. Special teams specifically had been formed to investigate last-known sites of American service personnel in Vietnam and Laos. For several years the teams had been searching for remains and evidence. While one of these teams was near the crash site of Hall's plane in Vietnam, an old man with a small bag spoke with the team members. He told them that many years previously, at the crash site he had found three teeth and some small bone fragments the size of the end of a fingernail. Mary Lou knew the old man could not have found the teeth at the crash site.

From conversations with Hall's wingman, Terry Heath; Terry's RIO, Phil Boughton; and LCDR Ernie Christensen, all of whom were at the scene of the attempted rescue of Hall, Mary Lou knew the details of the shootdown. Heath and Boughton saw Hall parachuting downward. Harley released his parachute. As he was running away from his landing position on the ground, the chute flew in the opposite direction of him. The separation of pilot from chute indicated that the chute had been released. Two big clips high on the flier's chest straps have to be opened consciously, manually, and actively for the aviator to be out of the chute harness. Chutes cannot be released automatically. For Harley to release his chute, he had to be alive and conscious. If he had been dragging the chute, both he and the chute would have been moving together—both in the same direction. For Mary Lou the fact that he had released his chute and was separated from it told her after he landed, he was alive and conscious.

Additionally the two crew members had different-colored chutes. The colors simplified the identification of the pilot in the front seat and the RIO in the backseat. Christensen had watched Hall's plane crash into the ground at a different location from what the Vietnamese man indicated. Hall was on ground about six miles away from the spot the man identified.

People throughout the Navy community knew Hall's professional reputation. Many people had told Mary Lou that Hall was alive and was being held in Vietnam. To Mary Lou returning POW's relayed messages through friends. Dr. Roger Shields from DIA called Mary Lou. She remembers his strong, emphatic voice, "He's there, Mary Lou. Don't you give up." Other high-ranking military officials—names Mary Lou refuses to have printed—also told Mary Lou that Hall still was alive in Vietnam. She knew he was not killed in the plane crash. He had to be accounted for.

Hall's three teeth were sent to the Central Identification Laboratory in Hawaii.[1] In January 1993 these were identified as the mortal remains of CAPT Harley Hall. Nothing else, however, was found—no big bones, only a few small pieces the size of the end of a fingernail—no clothing, no insignia, no personal items. *Does this make any sense?* Mary Lou asked herself again and again.

Mary Lou questioned whether DNA testing had been done. None had. She then asked for DNA testing to be done. The officials told Mary Lou that the testing of the teeth "didn't warrant the cost." Mary Lou was incredulous! Mary Lou was allowed to have testing done but only if she paid for the exam. She hired a highly recommended, private forensic odontologist to examine the teeth. A military escort delivered the three teeth to the forensic odontologist's office in Illinois.

The forensic expert was stunned, as was Mary Lou. They WERE three of CAPT Harley Hall's teeth! These three teeth, however, were not the teeth of the 34-year-old healthy pilot who was shot down, which is the condition in which they should appear if Hall indeed were killed at the crash site. The teeth showed years of periodontal disease, whereas CAPT Hall's dental x-rays taken in the fall of 1972, a few short months before his January 1973 capture, showed no periodontal disease. Dr. F.N. Powers Jr., forensic odontologist, in his report concluded that the primary tooth No. 5 was extremely important. No natural phenomenon exists in which tooth No. 5 could have been naturally exfoliated with this one exception.

Dr. Powers wrote his report:

> CAPT Hall lived far beyond the incident, thereby allowing severe periodontitis to occur and the bone resorption to become so severe that tooth No. 5 (possibly No. 6 and No. 9 as well) would become so loose that exfoliation could very easily have occurred. Also, the fractured palatal cusp could be explained by mechanical extraction. Two teeth, No. 5 and No. 6, show signs which are consistent with mechanical extraction. Tooth No. 9, comparatively, is an easy tooth to extract; therefore, not seeing external signs of a possible forceps is not alarming. I find it extremely interesting that DNA comparison has not been approached. The artifacts present on the teeth make acquisition of the teeth very suspicious to me. These three teeth do not draw the conclusion that CAPT Hall is dead and that these are his remains. To draw a conclusion that they alone represent the postmortem remains of an individual is, and would be, questionable at best; possibly, one might suggest absurd. Conclusion of death, at this time, with available evidence, I feel is inconclusive.
>
> Dr. F. N. Powers Jr., Forensic Odontologist[1]

Periodontist Dr. James Elliott of Fort Worth, TX, read Dr. Powers' report. He concurred that Powers' conclusions were based on the fact that the teeth appeared to have been extracted mechanically with pliers or some other type of equipment because of marks that appeared on the teeth. Additionally he pointed out that tooth No. 5 could not be extracted with pliers or a piece of equipment without years of periodontal disease. Tooth No. 5 has curved roots that will not break off, so the normal tooth cannot be extracted even with pliers or forceps. During a normal removal of this particular tooth with no incidence of periodontal disease, because of the root system, a periodontist cuts the tooth in half and then extracts it. "CAPT Hall had to have many years of periodontal disease for the tooth to be extracted in this manner," Dr. Elliott stated.[2]

CAPT Hall was shot down on the last day of the cease fire, so he had lived many years beyond the time that the POW's returned home during Operation Homecoming. Instead of closing the case, the existence of these teeth reopened it. The three teeth showed that Harley POSSIBLY COULD STILL BE ALIVE!

Another shock occurred when Mary Lou and other Vietnam War POW and MIA family members were given a one-time-only access to their relatives' classified files at Defense Intelligence Agency in Washington, DC. The protocol for viewing a file was quite strict. Only the primary next-of-kin could look at the file. Mary Lou, as Harley's widow and legal primary next-of-kin, could see his file. Their children could not go into the room with her. She was not allowed to take anything with her—no purse, no pencil, no paper. The file was on a table behind which stood a young naval officer. Mary Lou's friend Jean had remarried. Chuck, her new husband, an admiral, had made arrangements for both Mary Lou and Jean to go into the room together. They were not permitted to talk, nor were they to share files.

Two or three years before, Mary Lou had seen Harley's file. In the intervening years his file had grown in size until it was almost a foot thick because of the messages and the number of contacts, the number of spottings, the rumors heard, and the third-hand reports gathered. According to the data Hall was out there and alive. Harley's file contained intercepted radio messages recorded over the years. What was not new to Mary Lou was the information that after his capture Hall had been followed from North Vietnamese battalion to battalion. Information about a "Big Blue Angel" brought to Hanoi and paraded down the streets, probably to great jeers and derision and maybe even thrown rocks and fruit, shocked Mary Lou. Hall apparently was well-known to the Vietnamese because of the 1971 Blue Angels tour of Asia. Those newspaper and TV interviews he had given had returned to haunt him. The Vietnamese capture of a former Blue Angels Leader and top military pilot on the last day of the cease-fire was like money falling into their hands. Documents showed Hall had been interviewed by the Vietnamese.

During this look at Harley's files, however, Mary Lou saw that he also had been questioned by the Soviets. This definitely was new information. Seeing the declassified Soviet report showing that Harley had been interrogated in 1988 was another tremendous shock for Mary Lou. The files also reported a 1988 sighting of Hall in Laos. She could hardly breathe. Recognizing the importance of the file and its contents Mary Lou showed Jean the message. She wanted a witness. Of course the officer in charge told her she was not to be talking. She therefore immediately asked *him* for a copy of the document but did not receive one. (The protocol did allow her to speak to the officer.) In the next months she repeatedly asked DIA, Navy, and every other possible channel for a copy of the document. If she received an answer, she was told, "There was no document." The document was not in the file. It had somehow "disappeared". Both Mary Lou *and* Jean had seen and read that document. For YEARS Harley had been left alive in Vietnam!

What could she do? Go to Vietnam and look for him herself? He could be in Vietnam or in Laos or in Russia buried in some prison. Without a doubt if Harley were free to move around, he would get back to the States. He had to be held against his will. *Where? How could someone find Harley if he still were alive?* She had to find a way. Having received this new proof that he still could be alive, she had to find him! Mary Lou carried on her crusade for Harley.

Later in 1993 Mary Lou was told she could read a letter in front of the Congressional committee investigating POW/MIA matters. She immediately asked for the rules for the letter and its content as well as the protocol for the appearance. The trip would be at her expense. Further, the call inviting her to appear occurred only three days before the scheduled hearing—three days to marshal her argument, to write her case, to arrange for childcare, and to secure travel arrangements. She remembers those days as being a time God truly was with her. She believes He sat on her shoulder while she stayed up one entire night and wrote the letter. The result was a masterfully worded letter. Over and over she practiced reading the letter. Again and again she timed the letter. The letter was well under the allotted time. She titled the letter "Qualified Acknowledgment under Protest for Objectivity and Truth." She and four other relatives of POW's and MIA's spoke before Congress. Senator John Kerry and other Senators also were present. She read them the following report:

> Dear Sirs:
> In response to the recent recovery of three of CAPT Harley Hall's front teeth from the site of his downing and capture in 1/27/73, in Quang Tri Province, I would like the following to go on record:
> While I acknowledge these to be three of my husband's correctly identified teeth (confirmed by a dental

expert), I object most strenuously to the inference that they constitute evidence of death, and I by no means acknowledge or accept them as an accounting of the person of CAPT Harley H. Hall. As such, they represent not only insufficient evidence for case closure, but more importantly, BLATANTLY CONTRADICT ALL UNITED STATES GOVERNMENT ASSERTIONS AND INTELLIGENCE ON THE HARLEY HALL CASE. Specifically, various U.S. Agencies have consistently maintained that he could NOT POSSIBLY have died AT THAT SITE, i.e. Quang Tri, an inference drawn from multiple references of captivity elsewhere.

Apart from the obvious fact that adults frequently lost teeth, which was notorious among POW's, the condition of the teeth, the fact that they are front teeth, and especially the LOCATION of discovery, all point to a more obvious or plausible explanation. Namely, CAPT Hall was either punched, received a blow to the mouth by his captors, these teeth were extracted with some instrument like forceps or pliers, or fell out because of malnutrition and poor care.

As to the location of his alleged death:

1. NAVAL INTELLIGENCE: Naval Intelligence informed me two weeks after his downing that Harley had been captured—an absolute certainty based on first hand sensitive intelligence. It was the U.S. Government itself that had the information to change his status to Category I: Capture Confirmed. CAPT Hall remained in Category I POW status for a full seven years (1973-80) until such cases except Charles Shelton, USAF, were altered to "PFOD (Presumptive Finding of Death)."

2. DR. ROGER SHIELDS: It soon became evident

that Harley was not only captured, but had arrived at a prison site of some sort. I was personally told by POW/MIA expert Dr. Roger Shields that Harley's was one of the most compelling cases of capture he had ever reviewed. "They are holding your husband, Mrs. Hall, and one way or another they will have to answer for him and never settle for anything less."

3. THE NATIONAL SECURITY AGENCY: NAS files have subsequently revealed that CAPT Hall was tracked from battalion to battalion to a particular PRISON CAMP ON THE VIETNAMESE/LAOS BORDER, hence NOT in the Quang Tri Province.

4. DEFENSE INTELLIGENCE AGENCY REPORT: On 13 July, 1988, the DIA issued an analysis of Vietnamese reports to General Vessey about "an unrecoverable body in the Quang Tri area that had fallen into a trench." DIA analysis countered that this "answer" was totally unacceptable and that the SRV report was a concoction "implausible and in conflict with their known policies and practices regarding Americans." The area was heavily patrolled by North Vietnamese troops who would not have to resort to local villagers to account for an American downed under their noses. Next, local "witnesses" began to tell of an American body, allegedly Harley's, "buried there," but digging teams repeatedly found nothing. But now the sudden turnover of three teeth from Quang Tri is viewed as a "resolution," while in fact they in no way mitigate the U.S. Government's previous objection to this story and insistence that CAPT Hall could not have died there, let alone be buried there.

5. CLASSIFIED U.S. FILES: This summer I returned to Washington, DC to review all pertinent files

including classified material accessible to families. This reinforced my previous conclusion and added the STUNNING NEW REVELATION that Harley Hall had been INTERROGATED BY THE SOVIETS (which I hasten to point out, could not have happened had he "died" in the area where his teeth were allegedly lost and recovered twenty years later!). This is in startling contradiction to the U.S. Government's present bland acceptance of his "death" in the Quang Tri area shortly after being shot down.

6. REFUGEE STATEMENTS: I realize less credence is given to "hearsay" from Vietnamese, but it is no secret that about the time of my husband's downing and capture, there was frequent recounting and bragging about "the parading of a Big Blue Angel" in Vietnam and through Hanoi.

Cases of misidentification and case closings on insufficient evidence are not new or unique to my husband's case, but all the above shows me is that the United States Government's "highest national priority" in this area is to shorten if not eliminate the missing list and close the book on as many discrepancy cases as soon as possible, even if it means completely false burial of hundreds of Americans—all to expunge the past, achieve a hasty and slipshod "accounting," and facilitate lucrative and politically expedient relations with Hanoi.

As for the statement, "we have no information which would indicate CAPT Hall survived to become a captive of the Vietnamese," one need only consider every other agency cited here, and Harley's official POW status, to perceive a gross discrepancy and untruth.

Some cases are genuinely resolved. My close friend, Carleen Blackburn, received almost full skeletal remains of her husband (notably with FOUR FRONT TEETH MISSING). Other cases are not and perhaps never can or will be resolved. But the most unfortunate and painful of all are the FALSELY RESOLVED CASES. Thus, after twenty years of almost unbearable limbo and uncertainty, I may now face the worst case scenario: an eternal limbo, still not knowing. The three teeth only reinforce the intelligence on capture, while the U.S. Government prepares to call the case "unresolved" and cease even trying to account. Such a FALSE ANSWER IS WORSE THAN NONE, leaving me with less peace than before, not more!

I do not reject receiving the three teeth, nor will I take any legal action against their identification, because they are indeed Harley's teeth and constitute all I have of my husband at the present moment. Had they been presented in the spirit of further clues or evidence in Harley's case, and not as an unwarranted "accounting and resolution of death," I would even welcome them as one small clue to the mystery of what happened to him in captivity.

Be assured my protest does NOT stem from "wishful thinking," "hope against hope," or reluctance or refusal to accept death as an inevitable/probable outcome. For years, I have imagined, longed for and even dreamed of the day when I could hold a proper memorial service for Harley when his earthly remains could rest on U.S. soil. Then his children and I could experience the peace of knowing and begin to close the chapter of grief. But to grant burial with full military honors and a full size coffin to three front teeth would not only be ridiculous, but represent acquiescence in a lie.

Considering the above, I protest the closure of Harley's case in the strongest possible terms, and implore you to leave his name on the honored list of unaccounted for Americans, specifically of "focus" POW cases where he is listed in the first place. (Otherwise, his name will wrongfully appear on the "remains returned" list, and many thoughtful Americans will assume that this notorious case is finally resolved or settled). To do otherwise on the basis of incomplete and misleading "remains" of three teeth is a travesty and an affront to the truth, as well as yet another blow to the families who have fought so valiantly (and had their faith so badly shaken) in this cause. This is the least you owe to the men who served and those of us who have paid so high a price.

Signed,
Mary Lou Hall, wife
CAPT Harley Hall, USN

Mary Lou was about halfway through the letter when Senator John Kerry told her she was out of time. During her rehearsals she had timed the letter again and again. She knew she had not used up her time. "I have not used up my time," she argued with Kerry. He refused to allow her to continue. Mary Lou asked for the letter to be recorded in the Senate report. The letter changed nothing. The government was not moved to change its position. But Mary Lou would not give up. She had to find what happened to Harley.

Little did she know what else would be discovered.

[1] Powers.
[2] Elliott.

Chapter 16
Possible Live POW/MIA Documents Shredded

To find the truth about the missing POW/MIA's in Vietnam, Senator Bob Smith, a longtime POW advocate and Defense Intelligence Agency (DIA) critic, on the floor of the Senate on March 14, [1991] introduced legislation to create a Senate Select Committee on POW/MIA Affairs. Too much about the live POW issue was being kept secret, Smith charged. The Senate, he indicated, should exercise its authority and thoroughly investigate the issue once and for all:

> . . . As passed by the Senate, Smith's legislation called for a committee of twelve senators, six chosen by Majority Leader George Mitchell (D-ME) and six by Minority Leader [Bob] Dole. Because the Senate was controlled by the Democrats in 1991, a Democrat served as chairman and a Republican as vice chairman. The committee was empowered to subpoena documents and witnesses and was given approximately eighteen months to complete its investigation. Senator John Kerry, Democrat Senator from Massachusetts, was appointed Chairman of the Senate Select Committee on POW/MIA Affairs. Senator Mitchell chose Senators Bob Kerry of Nebraska, Charles Robb of Virginia, Tom Daschle of South Dakota, Harry Reid of Nevada . . . [and] Herb Kohl of Wisconsin. Dole would select Viet-

nam veterans Smith, McCain, and Hank Brown of Colorado, and Grassley, Helms, and Nancy Landon Kassebaum of Kansas.[1]

POW groups and family members such as Mary Lou were excited to learn of the Senate Select Committee on POW/MIA Affairs. The purpose of the committee not only encouraged these families but also bolstered their hopes that their men were not forgotten. The families and activists for the truth were convinced that Vietnam would be forced to tell the truth about U.S. POW/MIA's before it was awarded with relaxation of the U.S. trade embargo against Vietnam. At last she and other POW/MIA families would find definitive information about their loved ones.

The committee members first selected intelligence investigators to assist in gathering necessary data to make informed conclusions. Bill Hendon, one of the investigators, and Elizabeth A. Stewart wrote *An Enormous Crime: The Definitive Account of American POWs Abandoned in Southeast Asia*, a comprehensive chronicle of the working of not only the Senate Select Committee but also the investigators and the findings.

Smith, his top aide Dino Carluccio, and former U.S. Representative Bill Hendon quickly began developing an investigative work plan and assembling a team of intelligence investigators. Chosen to lead the effort was DIA Intelligence officer and attorney John Francis McCreary, the highly respected former member of the Tighe Task Force and principal author of the task force's final report. McCreary knew the POW issue inside and out and was highly recommended by Tighe, who told Smith that McCreary was one of the nation's finest and most accomplished intelligence officers.

Working with McCreary would be two army colonels, William "Bill" LeGro, who had served as chief intelligence at the U.S. embassy in Saigon during the period of 1973-1975 and had been among the last of the evacuated when the city fell, and Harold "Nick" Nicklas, who had just completed a distinguished career in Special Operations. Also serving would be civilians Robert "Bob" Taylor, a distinguished Middle East intelligence analyst formally assigned to the Office of the Secretary of Defense (International Security Affairs); John Holstein, Ph.D., a former House Foreign Affairs Committee Indochina expert and former Director of Asian affairs for the Agency of International Development (AID), and Hendon.

By Thanksgiving the investigative plan was almost complete. Smith and his men would request access to all intelligence (HUMINT, SIGINT, IMINT) relating to captured Americans received after January 27, 1973, by either the CIA, DIA, JCRC, the various military intelligence services, defense attaché offices worldwide, NSA and /or, DEA . . ..[2]

Soon after the committee meetings in the early 1990s, Mark Sauter and Jim Sanders wrote an exhaustive study of the POW/MIA situations, *The Men We Left Behind: Henry Kissinger, the Politics of Deceit and The Tragic Fate of POWs After the Vietnam War*. Their treatise gives a comprehensive study of the Senate Select Committee, the investigations, and the aftermath. McCreary, a long time DIA employee,

> was widely regarded as an exceptional intelligence officer, and he was reportedly one of the few U.S. Intelligence experts to predict Iraq's invasion of Kuwait . . .

McCreary began analyzing the human intelligence reports on U.S. POWs in Southeast Asia. Working with former Congressman Billy Hendon and Bob Taylor, another experienced investigator, McCreary sorted the POW reports and assigned or "clustered" them into the geographic areas where POWs had allegedly been seen. The idea was to focus on the information content of all reports, as opposed to the DIA's process of examining each report in minute detail with an eye to debunking it . . . . By analyzing the trends in 1,000 separate reports, the truth would emerge about whether U.S. POW's remained in Southeast Asia after the war.

As the investigators told their bosses in a special briefing: "This is a long-standing and proven method of analysis used by the U.S. Intelligence Community . . . the same method of analysis used by the U.S. Intelligence Community to track SCUD Missile firings by Iraq during the war. . . ."[3]

After the selection of the investigators, those men met to determine the best approach to analyze the numerous documents relative to the POW's and MIA's gathered from various avenues such as human intelligence (HUMINT).

In the intelligence business attempting to determine the veracity of a HUMINT report by checking for corroborative reports and comparing them as to event, location, time, circumstance, etc., with the information provided by the HUMINT source is called pattern analysis. The more a definite pattern develops in the reporting, i.e., same event, same time/period of time etc., the more likely it is that the sources are telling the truth. An extension of pattern analysis, cluster analysis, as old as intelligence analysis itself, involves the plotting of locations provided by sources on the map to test for corroboration. As common sense would indicate, if large numbers of reports from independent sources cluster around any given location there is a high degree of probability that the event the sources reported did in fact occur. And, correspondingly, a high degree of probability that the individual sources are credible, truthful reporters of that event. (Granted, individually these sources may include drug dealers, prostitutes, thieves, and other unsavory characters, but because these people independently reported the same event was taking place at the same place at the same location or around the same time or over a period of time, there is a high probability they are reporting truthfully about that event and are therefore, credible witnesses to that event.)

    McCreary and Hendon knew well that during the war, U.S. military intelligence officials had used cluster analysis frequently and effectively in Indochina. They knew, for example, that after wartime officials had received a mere handful of reports that American servicemen were being deployed as human shields at the Hanoi Thermal Power Plant, U.S. officials had declared, "In consideration of these reports, it is reasonable to conclude that POW's were being worked within the plant to deter aircraft from attacking it . . .." But McCreary and Hendon also knew—for reasons they were convinced could only be bad—that DIA had consistently refused to subject the postwar reports of live prisoners to cluster analysis, choosing instead to "analyze" and "investigate" each as if it were the only report ever received and then, in every case, rule that the source was either lying or had actually seen Russians, missionaries, etc. Knowing *all* of that, McCreary and Hendon chose cluster analysis as a way of showing that DIA's position could not possibly be valid.

McCreary, Hendon, LeGro, and Holstein, with periodic assistance from Nicklas, spent more than twenty-seven hundred hours vetting the postwar HUMINT. In the process, they found some 925 refuge reports they believed plausible and then began posting them with color coded plastic flags on a large map of Indochina. . . .. Looking at the map, the investigators saw that from Cao Bang to the Ca Mau in Vietnam and from Oudom Sai to Attopeu in Laos, the report clustered and clustered and clustered again of reported sightings of Americans. The refugees and other sources, the clusters said, were telling the truth.[4]

While the investigators worked to find well-substantiated truth, other committee members and politicians acted also. Hendon and Stewart wrote about John Kerry's report and public stance:

> Kerry had been chairman barely ten days when he announced to the press that he was leaving immediately for Indochina to investigate what he called "hot leads" on living POW's . . . .. After a series of meetings with Vietnamese leaders, Kerry returned to the United States and announced at a news conference that he strongly doubted there were any prisoners being held by the Communist governments of Southeast Asia . . . .. "I think the likelihood that a government is formally holding somebody is obviously tiny."[5]

Once again the families and those wanting to learn of the

fate of POW's and MIA's sought help:

> At the urging of the horrified activist families, Hendon met with Kerry to tell him of the huge volume of intelligence showing American POWs being held after the war by the Vietnamese and Laotian governments and to inform him exactly where the intelligence files were being stored and to request that he see to it that all of the intelligence be delivered to the committee so he and his fellow senators and members of the Senate Select Committee staff could examine it. Following a brief overview of the intelligence and where it was located, Hendon asked Kerry if he could show him some examples of the intelligence reports he had acquired in declassified form over the years. Kerry thanked Hendon for the offer but said his schedule was tight and it might be better if Hendon and Zwenig [Frances Zwenig, staff director of the Select Committee and chosen by Kerry] adjourned to the adjoining conference room to go over the material. To Hendon's surprise, he was only into his second or third declassified intelligence report when an obviously agitated Zwenig blurted out, "Listen, there is no need for us to go over these reports. The committee is not going to have time to go through all this type information. Our job is to put the war behind us and normalize relations. So there is no need to go over all this. But thank you for your interest and for taking the time to come by."[6]

Not deterred from their appointed task the investigators continued to analyze their findings and to prepare a report for the committee.

By the end of March 1992, the investigators were preparing to brief the committee's senators on findings of their study. They were required to present their findings first at the Senate Select Committee staff members briefing and were to present the information to the senators the next day. McCain had determined that an independent briefing of the senators be avoided at all cost. So in late March McCain staffer Mark Salter [McCain's chief aide on the POW/MIA issue] quietly contacted the Department of Defense (DOD), according to a Pentagon memo. According to Salter, the conclusion of the "intelligence" briefing was that Americans were still being held prisoner in Laos and Vietnam as late as 1989. Senator McCain felt it critical that DIA be present at the senators' briefing [the next day] to rebut the assertions . . ..[7]

The Senate Select Committee was initiated to find the truth about the POW/MIA's. This was to be an investigation and fact-finding task that included examining the findings of the DIA. DIA, the government intelligence agency in charge of investigations of missing U.S. military, is part of the Department of Defense (DOD). Why did McCain make the request that DIA be present? Such a request seemed a total reversal from McCain's opening statement at the Hearings of the Senate Select Committee on POW/MIA Affairs:

> I welcome this new opportunity to pursue answers that the families of our POW/MIA's have every right to expect and that the American people demand. I do not know if there are Americans in captivity in Southeast Asia. Until I have conclusive evidence one way or another, I will proceed on the assumption that there are. I

repeat: I assume there are live POW/MIA's in Southeast Asia until we have the fullest possible accounting for them.[8]

Another deviation from the original plan emerged, but McCreary remained optimistic and clear-sighted. Despite the directive from Kerry that a "dry-run briefing" be given the evening of April 8 to senior staffers from the various committee members' offices and Kerry's foreign-affairs specialists, "McCreary looked forward to this briefing like none he had ever presented. Never before had he seen better intelligence. Never before had he been more confident of his findings." McCreary and Hendon could not have imagined a more volatile reaction to their pre-briefing April 8. Hendon recorded the outcome: "At the conclusion of the briefing, the three Kerry staffers and Salter of McCain's office voiced strenuous objections to the investigators' findings regarding both the validity of the Gaines Report's findings and the fact that POW's remained alive as late as 1989."[9]

The reactions and results of the pre-briefing left both Hendon and McCreary incredulous, shaken, and even wary of the official briefing for April 9. They were well prepared, however, and knew their findings to be accurate, truthful, and important. Various accounts of the meeting concur on details. Hendon recorded the meeting:

> The select committee convened at 1:30 P.M. on April 9 [1992] in the U.S. Capitol's highly secure intelligence tank, Room S-407. Ten of the twelve committee members were in attendance, many accompanied by staff. A copy of the briefing text sat at each senator's place . . . . The atmosphere was charged, fueled by the presence of several officials from the DIA who had

been invited by Kerry and McCain.[10]

John McCreary and staff intelligence investigators displayed a six-foot-tall map of Indochina with 928 flags plotting locations of POW/MIA's. Hendon describes the ensuing events:

> McCreary had barely begun his presentation when McCain retook the floor and began hectoring the twenty-two-year DIA veteran . . . . McCreary made a game attempt to continue, but McCain had made it an adversarial contest . . . . After briefly presenting some of the intelligence and how it clustered, he turned the floor over to Hendon, who briefed for a short while and in turn recognized Taylor for his short briefing on satellite imagery.[11]

Similarly, Sauter and Sanders write of this all-important investigation and succeeding briefing. They, too, record that the investigators voiced the ominous pronouncement that "the intelligence indicates that American Prisoners of War have been held continuously after operation Homecoming [in early 1973] and remain[ed] in captivity in Vietnam and Laos as late as 1989."[12] The meeting with the committee probably was

> one of the most chaotic briefings in the history of U.S. intelligence. McCreary explained that his team had plotted the location of POW reports across Indochina. While "clearly outrageous, inflated, exaggerated or impossible reports" had been excluded from the analysis, some reports rejected by the DIA as "fabrications" had been included on the map. The reasoning was simple: since the Pentagon stood accused of falsely rejecting many reports, some of those rejected could really be

true, and they should be compared with other reports to see if a pattern emerged. Although this technique had been used with success in other areas of intelligence, it angered McCain who contested the use of any reports dubbed as "fabrications" by the DIA.[13]

Senator Kerry had a chance to be a real hero here, but Kerry's reaction was very strange. Sanders, who had been present at the Senate Select Committee Hearings, and Sauter gave this account:

> On 9 April 1992, the Chairman of the Senate Select Committee, Senator John Kerry of Massachusetts, in response to a protest by other members of the Senate Select Committee told the Select Committee members that "all copies" [of the POW Briefing] would be destroyed, along with the computer files of the briefing, McCreary wrote in his April 27 and May 3, 1992, Senate Memos . . .. One investigator said: "Kerry got scared when he found out what . . . was going on because this was not his agenda. His agenda was to open the ties with Vietnam. I think he was stunned . . . on the 9th of April when briefed that intelligence indicated that there were guys alive through 1989, (but later reports showed 1992). I think that just stunned him."[14]

According to Hendon's and Stewart's account in *An Enormous Crime*,

> Kerry then . . . directed that all copies of the classified briefing text held by the investigators or provided to the senators be passed to Kerry's staff so they could be counted, placed in a burn bag, and destroyed. No

copies, Kerry told those present, were to leave the room. "Welcome to Capitol Hill," Hendon told his much embarrassed and very angry comrade-in-arms as he and McCreary began gathering up the hundreds of overhead transparencies and files and placing them on carts for the return trip to the investigators' secure office in the basement of Russell . . . Zwenig shadowed the investigators' return to their office, and once all were inside, declared that Kerry had directed her to collect any extra copies of the briefing text in the investigators' safe. She also announced that Kerry had directed that all computer records relating to the briefing be destroyed in [her] presence. "So let's do it," she declared. Each investigator—McCreary, Hendon, LeGro, Holstein, and Nicklas—complied by deleting all files related to the briefing from their individual computers and showing Zwenig they had done so. Professing satisfaction, the staff director departed.

The original briefing and 14 copies reportedly were shredded on April 10, 1992.[15]

The investigators, however, were not lulled into a false contentment. They became fearful of possible investigations into their actions, albeit the destruction of the documents occurred at the directive of their reporting officials. On April 16, 1992, they asked for legal advice.

All six intelligence investigators of the Senate Select Committee requested an independent council to protect them from charges of criminal wrongdoing in connection with the destruction of the briefing files which may have been illegal under public records laws such as Title 18, United States Code, Section 20171.[16]

[A]ccording to McCreary, the committee's chief counsel, William Codinha, made light of the issue. "Mr. Codinha replied, 'Who's the injured party?' He was told, "The 2494 families of the unaccounted for US Servicemen, among others." Mr. Codinha then said, 'Who's going to tell them? It's classified,' recounted one of McCreary's memos.[17]

At 7:30, April 16, the Chairman of the Senate Select Committee (Senator John Kerry) convened a meeting with the intelligence investigators, who personally told him of their concerns that they might have committed a crime by participation in the destruction of the briefing texts at the order of the Staff Director. Senator Kerry told them that the issue [of document destruction] was "moot" because a copy of the briefing had been in the office of Senate Security "all along".[18]

McCreary, in his memos, claimed that one copy of the briefing was indeed in the Office of Senate Security by that time, but it had been placed there at 1:07 p.m. on April 16th.

In other words, all the original copies had been destroyed. But when destroying the briefings sparked controversy, Senator John McCain produced an extra, presumably bootlegged version of the briefing and placed it in the Senate Security Office seven days later on April 16, 1992 at 1:07 p.m. to cover up the destruction of the documents, McCreary reported in his April 27, 1992, and May 3, 1992, Senate Memo.[19]

The deliberate destroying of the documents remained a concern for the investigators. In his letter dated May 8, 1992 the Legal Counsel, Michael Davidson, United States Senator, consulted by the Senate Select Committee Intelligence Investigators, seemed to give a pass concerning the destruction of the POW/MIA documents. But was the entire situation a "moral issue of honesty versus dishonesty", or a legal question? Even though they might get away with it legally, were the senators honest in shredding documents of U.S. fathers, sons, husbands, and brothers of POW/MIA families possibly still alive in Vietnam in 1992? The three teeth of CAPT Harley Hall recently had returned home with forensic testing indicating he possibly could still be alive. Therefore, were all or some of the POW/MIA's that intelligence showed possibly alive still alive also? Before these recorded activities, at a hearing in Washington Mary Lou had tried to speak to Senator Kerry to tell him about CAPT Hall. As she was reading her letter to the committee and the senators, Kerry realized he was being given information that CAPT Hall was possibly still alive. Kerry told Mary Lou her time was up and would not let her continue. Did Kerry not want to hear the facts she began to present to him and others present? Did he ever read the letter she left for him and the committee?

Hendon reported additional actions of the committee.

> Senate Select Committee Investigators met again on June 3, 1992, to file official estimates of the numbers of American POW/MIAs their latest intelligence showed were possibly still being held alive by the Vietnamese and Laos governments at that time . . . . The select committee descended into chaos . . . . In mid-June, Kerry first revoked Hendon's security clearance . . . and then Carluccio's . . . . Hendon, knowing he would be unable to proceed with . . . activity that required access to the intelligence, gave Smith notice of his intention to resign and began cleaning out his office. Carluccio . . . also cleaned out his office at the committee's headquarters suite in the Hart Building and moved back into Smith's suite in the Hart Building.[20]

These actions sent a message to others on the committee. If they wished to keep their government jobs, they had to keep silence as Kerry and the committee wished.

Leaks of the classified information from the Senate Select Committee to newspapers about POW/MIA live-sightings and POW distress signals seen on the ground by satellite imagery began to occur. Kerry's staff sent a memo to committee members to determine who leaked the classified information.[21]

As early as May 1992 the press picked up the actions of members of the committee, investigators, and politicians. Tommy Denton, senior editorial writer and columnist for the Fort Worth *Star-Telegram,* in his May 14, 1992, column penned the following words:

> Under whose authority were documents removed? Where are leaks going? I was notified that because of internal squabbling between folks in the Committee staff and some who were on the other staff—disputes over process at the staff level—leaving people with the impression that this thing was about to hit the shoals. I was told about the meeting in which Sen. McCain went off in the area of demanding investigation for fraud and demanding that the DIA be brought in rather than have independent judgments of the investigative staff on the documents. As a result of that, the investigators began to sense an ambush—in other words that the integrity of the investigation was about to be compromised.
>
> I have not talked to the investigators, so what I'm telling you is something from people who have reason to say. In defense, stuff was going to start flying out of there to protect the integrity of the investigation—because there were internal forces to stifle the investigation. I knew that leaks were imminent over a month

ago—I knew on 4/9.

If a Senator charged with getting (to) the bottom of this is using obstructionist measures . . . . Why have DIA there looking over the investigators' shoulders? Why not use the expertise you have? I'll buy that.

Similarly, Jack Anderson began research concerning the MIA issue. He directed his investigations toward Kerry as the chairman of the Select Committee. The memo from Deborah De Young to Kerry delineates the conversation with Anderson and the questions Anderson left for Kerry. The memo, in its entirety, follows.

To: Senator John F. Kerry
Senator Bob Smith
From: Deborah De Young
Date: May 4, 1992
RE: Jack Anderson column

Michael Binstein, Jack Anderson's co-author, called around 4 p.m. today. His telephone number is 944-3030. He needs answers by 12 noon May 5 for the first in a series of stories he's writing about the MIA issue.

Here is a near-verbatim transcript of his questions.

The column is about what's going on behind-the-scenes with the committee.

1. Was there a shouting match on the plane to Vietnam between Senator Kerry and either Senator or Mr. Hendon? [I said Hendon was not on the plane; he said Hendon was somewhat involved].

2. Does Senator Kerry believe as of today that there is evidence of live American MIAs in Vietnam or Laos?

Questions on the April 9 briefing: We've had access to certain Committee documents, and after reviewing

Committee staffers, there have been allegations that (a) Kerry has ordered the destruction of the documents; (b) Kerry has condoned McCain's leaking of the documents to DIA; (c) McCain was disruptive, unruly and rude during the April 9 briefing; (d) Kerry is apparently upset with McCain.

I also want to find out about an incident toward the end of the April 9 meeting involving Kerry's chief of staff, Frances. Apparently she had a confrontation with Senator Smith, who was interrogating—pretty roughly—the DIA people. It was just Smith and the DIA people left in the briefing. She and others thought that Senator Smith was being a little abusive. DIA officials thought the tone of the questioning had become abusive. At one point she told them they didn't have to take it . . . and they left. Well, maybe not exactly at that point, but they didn't leave happy campers.

Billy Hendon believes, according to people who are familiar with his thinking, that many members of the Committee, including Senator Kerry, are wittingly or unwittingly involved in a cover-up of information. That they either won't look or they look the other way at evidence of live MIA sightings. That there is a whitewash in progress—I told you about the document destruction of files Sen. Kerry has ordered and subjected them to great civil or criminal trouble. That is why they are forcing the hearing this Thursday.

Why did Senator Kerry allow Billy Hendon such a large role on the Committee? What does he think about the job he's doing? Does he believe that Billy and the people that work with him on the Committee (even though he's a designee . . .) are seeing their work get sabotaged by McCain and the DIA?

I'm telling you this as it's been reported to me. These are the allegations that I'm originating. You understand that.

I'm interested in the scope of Ross Perot's contribution to the Select Committee. My information is that he was interviewed in Dallas by two of your investigators. I'd like you to characterize what his contributions have been.

Also, I'd like some statement from Senator Kerry about his evaluation about how the Committee has been doing. Does he think it's closer to finding the truth and will he allow an extension like Dino is proposing. Apparently, Kerry is going to block a six-month extension which people like Dino are pushing. Is that true or not?

That's about the gist of it—just do the best you can. By 11 tomorrow? This is the first piece I'm doing, but it won't be the last. I have a deadline tomorrow. About noon is the most I can push it.
CC: Frances A. Zwenig
Dino L. Carluccio
L. William Codinha[22]

Another delegation flew to Vietnam. Whether the mission was to ascertain numbers and veracity of various sightings and reports of POW's and possible MIA's or to substantiate claims of those not embracing the investigative reports can be surmised from accounts given by Sauter and Sanders.

On July 14-15, 1992, Kerry's staff director [Zwenig] traveled to Vietnam with Pentagon officials . . .. During a talk with Le Bang, Hanoi's top expert on the U.S., Zwenig made a stunning statement concerning Kerry's expectations. She said Senator

Kerry believes that the Vessey cases [POW/MIA cases predicted to have the greatest chance of survival] can be solved by identification of remains, through records, from witnesses of deaths, or some combination of these . . . the Pentagon reported in a cable to the U.S. In other words, Zwenig gave Hanoi a road map on how to settle the POW issue without providing all evidence in its possession. More importantly, she never mentioned the return of living Americans as a requirement for resolving the issue.[23]

Intelligence experts reported no satellite or drone intelligence was used to check the locations after Senate Select Committee investigators reported 650-850 POW/MIA's possibly remained alive (according to the Senate Select Committee Intelligence Investigators). Why wasn't this method of gathering intelligence employed? Why not do this?

Official select committee reports filed with Senate publications, writings, and logs of activity provide insight into the complicated task as well as the conflicting investigation methods and ensuing findings. As early as 1991 the top-ranking official for the POW/MIA office tendered his resignation. He elaborated on his numerous reasons for his actions.

>Colonel Millard A. Peck resigned his position as the Chief of the Special Office of Prisoners of War and Missing in Action alluding to the fact that any report which found its way there [to the POW-MIA Headquarters] would quickly disappear into a "black hole."
>
>Practically all analysis is directed to finding fault with the source. Rarely has there been any effective, active follow-through on any of the sightings, nor is there a responsive "action arm" to routinely and aggressively

pursue leads.

There was, and still is, a refusal by any of the players to follow normal intelligence channels in dealing with the POW-MIA Office.

The dark side of the issue was particularly unsettling because of the persistent rumors and innuendoes of a Government conspiracy, alleging that U.S. military personnel had been left behind to the victorious communist governments in Vietnam, Laos, and Cambodia, and that for "political reasons" or running the risk of a second Vietnam War, their existence was officially denied. Worse yet was the implication that DIA's Special Office for POWs and MIAs was an integral part of the effort to cover the entire affair up so as not to embarrass the Government nor the Defense Establishment.

Heading up the Office had not been pleasant. My plan was to be totally honest and forthcoming on the entire issue and aggressively pursue innovative actions and concepts to clear up the live-sighting business, thereby refurbishing the image and honor of the DIA. I became painfully aware, however, that I was not really in charge of my own office, but was merely a figurehead or whipping boy for a larger and totally Machiavellian group of players outside the DIA. What I witnessed during my tenure as the cardboard cut-out "Chief" of POW-MIA could be euphemistically labeled as disillusioning.[24]

Colonel Peck's report was in the Senate Select Committee Hearings Report; therefore, McCain and Kerry would have been aware of his situation and how the DIA would react when DIA personnel were allowed into the committee meeting on April 9, 1992.

The Report of the Select Committee on POW/MIA Affairs, United States Senate, which was published January 1993, stated that "The Committee's main conclusion was that there is no compelling evidence that any American POW's are alive today in Southeast Asia." Two senators, however, disagreed. The Senate Select Committee allowed Mr. Sheetz of the DIA to give the final summation of the DIA report and allowed others to recount reasons POW/MIAs could not be alive in 1989 or 1992. On the other hand, the Committee's report stated clearly and unequivocally the following information concerning DIA:

> DIA's office had historically been
> • Plagued by a lack of resources;
> • Guilty of over-classification;
> • Defensive toward criticism;
> • Handicapped by poor coordination with other elements of the intelligence community;
> • Slow to follow up on live-sightings and other reports and frequently distracted from its basic mission by the need to respond to outside pressures and requests;
>
> In addition, several of those who reviewed the workings of DIA during this period also faulted DIA analytical process and referred to a "mindset to debunk" live-sighting reports.
>
> Several Committee members expressed concern and disappointment that, on occasion, individuals within the DIA have been evasive, unresponsive, and disturbingly cavalier.[25]

With this information from Peck on record, the fact that the Senate Select Committee allowed this branch of the DIA into its meeting to defend its position and allowed it to help write the final Committee report stands incomprehensible. The Committee's charge was to investigate the DIA and other organizations for truth and for incompetence in not finding POW/MIA's. Since 1973 DIA had received 15,559 live-sighting reports in Vietnam and Indochina but never found any live POW/MIA's. Others went to Vietnam to seek information. Kerry went at least twice and sent his staff officer once. On November 16, 1992, Kerry's delegation traveled to Vietnam. It was accompanied by JTF-FA commander Major General Needham; again the group was looking for document resolution or remains of POW's. No live POW/MIA's were required.[26]

When Senator Bob Smith introduced legislation to create a Senate Select Committee on POW/MIA Affairs in March 24, 1991, a committee to find the fate of missing POW/MIA's, certainly he could not imagine how these unbelievable events could occur. Finding the fate became covering up the truth!

Facts from message traffic and the Russian document show irrevocably that Blue Angels Leader CAPT Harley Hall was left alive in Vietnam and possibly was alive for years. Were the other POW's alive also? Were they living on meager amounts of food, enduring horrible living conditions, and as prisoners working in fields for the Vietnamese? Would their families ever learn the truth of their status? Was Mary Lou to live forever in this emotional chaos and uncertainty?

[1]Hendon 403, 405.
[2]Hendon 407.
[3]Sauter and Sanders 353.
[4]Hendon 415.
[5]Hendon 405.
[6]Hendon 405-406.
[7]Sauter 353.
[8]*Hearings before the Senate Select Committee on POW/MIA Affairs.* 14.
[9]Hendon 418.
[10]Hendon 417.
[11]Hendon 419.

[12] Sauter and Sanders 355.
[13] Sauter and Sanders 354.
[14] Sauter and Sanders 355.
[15] Hendon 419.
[16] Sauter and Sanders 356.
[17] Sauter and Sanders 355-56.
[18] Sauter and Sanders 356.
[19] Sauter and Sanders 355-56.
[20] Hendon 432.
[21] Denton.
[22] Senate Select Committee.
[23] Sauter and Sanders 357-358.
[24] Senate Select Committee.
[25] Senate Select Committee 191-192.
[26] McConnell 399.

Chapter 17
More Documents Shredded

In 1993 another unsettling and disturbing story "shook the United States badly". On January 2, 1993, Stephen Morris, a Harvard researcher, discovered a shocking document in the newly opened Archives of the Central Committee of the Communist Party in Moscow. During the Vietnam War the Soviets had been Hanoi's chief advisers and suppliers. The Central Committee Archives afforded a unique opportunity to get a look at what happened "on the other side of the hill" (referring to those not part of government). On April 10, 1993, the Russian newspaper *Izvestia* broke Morris's story; articles in the *New York Times*, *Washington Times*, *Boston Magazine*, and other news media followed. The lengthy article written by David Chanoff in *Boston Magazine* certainly strengthened the *Izvestia* story's impact and presented a comprehensive study of Morris and his findings. Chanoff's article not only chronicles Morris's findings but also describes the aftermath of Morris's conversations with government officials and ensuing actions by the government—conversations that concerned POW/MIA matters.[1]

Chanoff carefully describes Morris's purpose for being in Moscow to conduct his research and tells of Morris's credentials as a Soviet-Vietnam scholar as well as Morris's decision-making process for sharing the contents of this find.

> Morris reassured himself that the reports in it had been prepared by Soviet political and intelligence sources and been signed off by high-ranking Soviet

officials, including Marshal Ogarkov, the chief of staff. He noted that the former head of the Soviet military intelligence, Pyotr Ivashutin, had signed an "Executive Summary" of the POW document for the party's Central Committee and that the Central Committee had ordered a special report on it for the Politburo. Clearly the Soviet hierarchy believed the information was genuine.[2]

Because Morris did not remember the exact number of POW's returned, he called two friends in the U.S. The number of returnees was 591. But the document he read gave the number as 1,205 Americans in prisons. This report indicated that more than 600 American prisoners who were alive in September 1972 had not been returned during Operation Homecoming.

Sauter and Sanders noted an affirming response to the Quang report.

Former Director of the DIA, Retired Lieutenant General Eugene F. Tighe, said what the DIA already knew. "We had a list [of POWs in 1971] that was really significantly larger than those who came back . . . [W]e had been expecting a lot more people. It was terribly shocking. Finally, we are getting proof of what we said —the numbers [in the Soviet report] don't surprise me at all."[3]

Chanoff continues the narrative about Morris and the information he found. Harvard-based political scientist Stephen Morris theorized "that the United States and its southern ally may have been within a hair of winning" the military conflict—that in fact the war was all but won in 1972, had we only known it. For this reason he was doing "research in the newly opened archives of the Central Committee for the Communist Party . . . Morris had never been active in POW/MIA affairs . . .. There was not a doubt in his mind that somehow he had to make public what he had found. But he wished the burden of delivering this message had fallen on anyone but him . . .. In mid January, Morris was on Delta flight 31 back to New York. He had considered announcing his find to the *New York Times* upon landing. But on the plane he discussed the situation with Mark Kramer, another Harvard scholar who had been working in the archives. Kramer argued that he ought to go to the government. "What if any of them are still alive?" he asked.[4]

Morris's document find was a 25-page report marked *Extremely Secret*. Section three of the report was from the deputy chief of the general staff of the Vietnamese army and was presented by Lieutenant General Tran Van Quang at a meeting of the Politburo (Communist Party) on September 15, 1972 (four months, 12 days before the Vietnam War ended).

"Today," General Quang said, "I will also report to you on the questions of American prisoners of war. Up to the present time the number of American POWs in the Democratic Republic of Vietnam has not been published. We are keeping the number a secret. At today's meeting of the Politburo I will report to you, Comrades, the exact number of American POWs taken up to now on the fronts of Indochina—that is to say, North Vietnam, South Vietnam, Laos, and Cambodia—is 1,205."[5]

Other *New York Times* articles contain more of the document Morris found. Christine Bohlen quoted Quang's report:

1,205 American prisoners of war located in the prisons of North Vietnam—this is a big number. Officially until now, we published a list of only 368 prisoners of war. The rest we have not revealed. The Government of the U.S.A. knows this well, but it does not know the exact number of prisoners of war, and can only make guesses based on its losses. That is why we are keeping the number of prisoners of war secret, in accordance with the Politburo's instructions.[6]

The Quang Document itself, published in the *New York Times* the same day Bohlen's article appeared, showed not only the Soviet Union's involvement in the Vietnam War but also the conditions both North Vietnam and the Soviet Union at the end of the hostilities expected about the prisoners of war. Quang continued his report with expectations and planned actions.

The question of the prisoners of war, as is well known, we intend to resolve in the following manner:
1. The Government of the U.S.A. must demonstrate compliance, that is, to a cease-fire and to remove Nguyen Van Thieu, and then both sides will set about discussion of the question of the return of the prisoners of war to the Nixon Government.
2. At this time, until the American side settles the foregoing problem, we will be able to free only a few of the fliers from the number of progressive orientation. Nixon cannot stand in the way of the return of these fliers to the motherland . . ..
3. Nixon must compensate North Vietnam for the enormous losses which the destructive war caused.
These are the principles on the basis of which we

are able to resolve the question of the American prisoners of war.[7]

According to Quang, therefore, as early as September, 1972, the Politburo (the Vietnamese Communist Party Leadership) decided to keep and use American POW's to bargain with the U.S. Government for reconstruction aid for Vietnam.

> Morris, after much deliberation on his moral obligation and his academic and personal lives, decided to take his findings to the government administration.
> Over the next few days, senior Soviet expert scholar Richard Pipes of Harvard and national security adviser Zbigniew Brzezinski examined the document and judged it authentic. It seemed clear to them that this was a valid Soviet archival document. The chances of it having been planted or fabricated were negligible . . . .
> In a meeting in Berger's office on February 11, 1993, Morris handed the deputy security adviser a memorandum that detailed the essential information contained in the document . . . . "We'll see what we can find out about it," Berger said. "I'll be back to you in a week."
> Over the next few days, Morris was contacted several times by people from the Defense Department, including Acting Deputy Secretary for POW/MIA affairs Ed Ross . . . . Despite Morris's persistent efforts to reach Berger, he did not call back until March 17, five weeks after their meeting. And then it was only with a question about whether the 1,205 Americans mentioned in the report might have included captured South Vietnamese or other allied troops. Morris told him the language was clear; it meant only Americans.[8]

Obviously President Clinton and his staff must have believed the document to be accurate, because suddenly a three-day horrendous shredding of thousands of U.S. POW/MIA documents, including the many live sightings and human intelligence, occurred. On April 8, 1993, *Washington Times* reporter Bill Gertz reported the horrifying, alarming actions.

General Colin Powell, Chairman of the Joint Chiefs of Staff, ordered an investigation into the destruction of thousands of POW files on servicemen missing in Southeast Asia. They were pulverized last month in a refrigerator-sized shredding machine at the U.S. Embassy in Bangkok, Thailand. The files contained information that had not been duplicated and included live-sighting reports, data from unresolved cases and handwritten investigator's notes. They contained reports from field agents who looked for POW/MIAs in Vietnam and Indochina. The files containing possible live-sightings of POW/MIAs and were destroyed by orders from Maj. General Thomas Needham on March 25-27, 1993. "They destroyed informal notes and memoranda—the meat of actual investigations," said Maj. Petrie, a former Special Forces Officer.[9]

Together with the shredding of the reports given to the Select Senate Committee on POW/MIA Affairs, all evidence of live POW/MIA's had been destroyed—not by American foes but by the American government officials.

Although some Vietnam POW/MIA experts disagreed with the authenticity of Morris's find, many government officials, however, believed it accurate, so much so that it set off a storm of Vietnam POW/MIA document shreddings. Why the shredding of POW/MIA documents unless the documents contained proof that many POW/MIA's still were being held alive in Vietnam long after the war had ended and possibly might be alive? Did government officials not want to answer for the POW numbers Quang's report contained—numbers confirmed by various DIA and investigators who prepared the Select Senate report? What did this information do to or for the families? What about Hall and his fellow prisoners? Where were they? Why were the POW's being discounted as if they were figments of imagination?

[1] Chanoff 82.
[2] Chanoff 84-88.
[3] Sauter and Sanders 357-358.
[4] Chanoff 84-5, 109.
[5] Chanoff 84.
[6] Bohlen, A1.
[7] Vietnam's 1972 Statement A6.
[8] Chanoff 109-10.
[9] Gertz A5.

Chapter 18

Huge Money Deal

On June 16, 1993, the *Boston Herald* published an article about a financial transaction relative to American investments in Vietnam. Stewart C. Forbes, CEO of Colliers International, announced that John Forbes, Senator John Kerry's cousin, helped broker a $905-million contract for a deep seaport in Vietnam. At that time Colliers' deal was the largest investment in Vietnam. The article quoted Forbes: "Talks that might have led to normalization of relations between the United States and Vietnam have repeatedly foundered on the question of Americans missing in action."[1]

But this time relations with Vietnam would not fail. At John Kerry's request the Senate Select Committee's 500-page report and all the computer investigative files were destroyed. The archived POW/MIA files stored in Bangkok for more than 20 years were shredded. This action likely was ordered by President Clinton's office. The Quang document which Morris discovered during his Moscow archival research Morris had given only to Clinton's administrative office.

Hanoi, too, had reeled from the release of the document. The new government in Vietnam wanted to establish trade relations with the U.S. and to secure loans from the International Monetary Fund. Hanoi was able to offer many reasons it could not have held these POW's and reasons the Soviet Quang Document could not be true. For many years and on many occasions the Vietnamese had tried to exchange POW's for money from the United States; however, now that the Vietnamese were offered loans from the International Monetary Fund, they averred they no longer had POW's. With an investment of the magnitude of Colliers International, Hanoi could pay off its $140 million to the International Monetary Fund and simultaneously gain access to much-larger overseas credit markets.

Lifting the embargo with Vietnam was an important step in making the money deal work. When on September 13, 1993, President Clinton lifted part of the embargo on Vietnam, billions of dollars became available for real-estate development loans from the World Bank and International Monetary Fund. Three months afterward American companies were permitted to obtain from the World Bank and the International Monetary Fund loans for construction projects in Vietnam. Forbes' four-year project did not begin until the next year—1994.[2] On February 4, 1994, President Clinton, surrounded by Senator John Kerry, Senator John McCain, other members of Congress, and business leaders, officially announced that the United States was lifting the 19-year economic embargo against Vietnam.

These unsettling actions with all those shredded documents blowing in the wind depict Washington politics at its absolute worst. What happened to CAPT Hall and the many other POW/MIA's? What can we, as Americans, do? What can we do to find the truth? What can we do to accept the truth? How can we ensure such travesties never, ever occur again?

[1] Knell O32.
[2] Ibid.

Epilogue

Despite the political machinations, the financial deals, and the diplomatic relationships between nations, the search for POW's and MIA's continued. For families such as those of Carleen, Jan, Jean, and Mary Lou and others in similar situations, the POW/MIA issue was not a closed subject. For many in government circles the issue was far from closed.

In 1999, 26 years after Hall's shoot-down, Mary Lou learned that the military intended to bury Harley's teeth in Arlington National Cemetery. The burial would allow the Department of Defense to list Hall as "remains returned". For many years Mary Lou had not accepted the three teeth because of the provisions attached to accepting them. If Mary Lou were to accept the teeth, that would allow the government officials to write Hall off as "remains returned", conduct his military funeral, and close his case. Mary Lou believed a funeral for three teeth was not the right thing to do. The funeral would be a sham and a mockery. She often told the officials that "three teeth do not Harley make."

Jim Maslowski, Harley and Mary Lou's long-time friend, still was in the Navy but was stationed in Washington, DC. He was to visit in San Diego a few days after Mary Lou learned of the proposed funeral for Harley. During that visit he and Mary Lou met for lunch. She talked with him about the proposed burial and shared her idea for what to do with the teeth. She kept Harley Stephen's and Heather's baby teeth in a small burl wood box. This tiny, three-inch-by-one-and-a-half-inch box seemed the logical place to house Harley's teeth. She then would give the box to Larry Pruitt, a builder and developer in charge of the new building in Vancouver—a building to be named for Harley and dedicated to his memory. The box could be put in the foundation. Jim liked Mary Lou's idea. He made necessary arrangements with the Navy so no funeral happened. He spoke with Pruitt. He also ascertained that placing the teeth in the foundation was legal. Through his actions Mary Lou finally achieved peace. He had told her, "You can't have what you want, but you can have peace."

Some months later Mary Lou and Jim went to Travis Air Force Base near San Francisco; there they retrieved the teeth from the mortuary. Jim was pleased to help Mary Lou. At the mortuary both Jim and Mary Lou had to sign for the teeth. Jim's hands shook as he accepted the small plastic bag, which was stapled shut. The entire process took a toll on him. Like Mary Lou he had lived many years with the memory of Hall. During change of commands on ships he always mentioned Hall as one whose service should be remembered. But Mary Lou felt differently about the teeth. These three brown teeth did not seem connected with Harley at all. She repeated, "Three teeth do not Harley make." She took the teeth and put them in her purse.

When they left Travis AFB, Mary Lou and Jim drove into San Francisco to meet Heather, Mary Lou's daughter, who worked and lived in the city. The three of them then flew to Vancouver, Harley's hometown. In Vancouver Harley Stephen joined his mother and sister. Soon the teeth would find their proper place.

The beautiful H.H. Hall Professional Building contains pictures and life-size glass etchings of Hall. The contents of the glass display case includes Hall's medals, a model of his F-4 Phantom Fighter Jet, and his Blue Angels flight suit and helmet, along with other uniforms and memorabilia which Mary Lou donated. Many of Hall's family members, members of

Hall's Blue Angels Team, and friends traveled long distances to attend the ceremony—RADM Ernie Christensen, Blue Angel and former commander of the *USS Ranger*; Steve Shoemaker; Kevin O'Mara and his wife, Mary Russell O'Mara; Bill Beardsley; Frank Mezzadri, former Blue Angel and Hall's best friend; and Hall's wingman, Terry Heath. RADM Jim Maslowski, former Blue Angel and former Commanding Officer of *USS Kitty Hawk*, spoke at the July 14, 2000, dedicatory ceremony. Linda, Harley's sister who had been invited to try out for the New York Metropolitan Opera but chose the life of a missionary teacher, at Mary Lou's request sang *The Impossible Dream*. Mezzadri spoke and told fun stories that made everyone feel as if Harley were right there with them. The narratives of some of Harley's antics had everyone laughing. Then Maslowski gave his tribute to Harley.

>CAPT Hall was a patriot, pilot, and warrior. He was my Blue Angels flight leader in 1970 and 1971 when I was an over-confident young lieutenant, convinced I was going to live forever. He first taught me humility, but then he went on to give me lessons about leadership and life that I attempted to emulate every day of my naval career. He taught me to strive for perfection in everything I did, to encourage and challenge my subordinates as he challenged me, and never to compromise my standards or my beliefs to avoid controversy or personal inconvenience. Hall was a naval aviator's aviator, a "good stick," and a gentleman. He led by example and by making us work for his approval. In attracting us to be just like him, he was a role model extraordinaire and a mentor who inspired all who had the privilege to walk in his shadow. When his F-4 Phantom launched off the deck of the *USS Enterprise* on the morning of 27

January 1973, headed for Quang Tri Province, he had everything to live for: a lovely wife, a beautiful daughter, and a soon-to-be-born son; the end of the war already determined in its date and hour; and a most promising career in Naval Aviation. But no matter what the dangers that day would bring, there was no question of not giving his all to accomplish the mission. It was this uncompromising sense of duty that brought him back for another pass at a cluster of North Vietnamese supply vehicles, and it was during this valiant and courageous effort that he was lost on the very last day of combat, 27 January 1973.

CAPT Hall would be 63 in 2000 and most certainly a retired four-star admiral. The Vietnam Veterans Memorial in Washington, DC—The Wall—bears the name of 58,214 individuals who made the ultimate sacrifice of giving their life for America in the Vietnam War. You can find CAPT Hall's name on Panel O1W, Line 112.

Yes, some say we "lost" the battle for South Vietnam, but in a much larger perspective, we won a global war for much higher stakes. Although the "Domino Theory" is often dismissed, two dominoes—Laos and Cambodia—did, in fact, fall and were taken over by Vietnamese Communists. Land once owned by the people is now owned by their government, which assigns quotas of rice or whatever they produce that they must meet on land they once owned. We now see looking through a rear-view mirror, that it was only the willingness of the free world—particularly the United States—to put lives and treasures on the line in Vietnam that slowed and eventually reversed that tide, and kept countries like Thailand, Malaysia, Singapore, Indonesia, and perhaps even the Philippines and Taiwan from falling, too. The many men who made individual sacrifices like CAPT Hall, who bravely did their duty—because it was their duty, are <u>heroes</u> who have protected the many freedoms we have today in America.

At the dedication ceremony, Mary Lou made peace with Harley. As if he were beside her, she told him she had done all she could do. She had to let it go. After that date she didn't carry on the crusade for his return.

According to the official forensic odontologist's report which was based on periodontal analysis, Hall's three teeth had been manually extracted or knocked out but had remained in his mouth for at least three- to three-and-a-half years after his shootdown. The reports in Hall's DIA file proved that Hall perhaps was alive 20 years after his capture. Ensuing investigation provided veracity to claims of many who believed not all American Prisoners of War and those Missing in Action had been returned. For many Americans Hall's face is the symbol of thousands possibly alive in Vietnam, because he was known to be alive many years after the cease fire in 1973. The uncertainty of his years after his shootdown stands amidst the surety of his captivity extending well beyond the 1973 negotiations. Those three teeth proved a valid point: Mary Lou was right in her fight with the government. The government had turned its back on these men and left them there in captivity. Only an act of God would bring Harley home. Mary Lou's fight for the return of POW's and MIA's was not in vain. Remaining true to her convictions Mary Lou Hall would not agree to bury Hall's teeth in Arlington Cemetery as the military requested, because she never knew when or even whether Hall died. That sad day in 1973 at the graveside service for Skip Umstead, Mary Lou gathered her resolve and determined that she would and could move forward. She did.

Today, Mary Lou continues her quiet, simple life—a testimony to her strength, her character, her faith in God. During her children's growing-up years she enjoyed every minute of their numerous activities—including field trips, ball games and track meets, and performances. They are God's gift to her, she says tenderly. She saw that both children were well educated and were prepared for independent, successful adult lives. Heather received her undergraduate degree from Princeton and a master's in business administration and a master of science in accounting from San Diego University. She works in the financial industry in San Francisco. Harley Stephen, a graduate of Johnson and Wales Culinary Institute with a bachelor of science in hotel and restaurant management as well as chef's credentials, is an executive chef in a private club in Santa Barbara, CA. He and his wife, Arica, married in September 2008.

Mary Lou continued to live in San Diego among friends both she and Harley had known and new ones she made after his shootdown. Her large family remained close in relationships with her. She enjoyed a social life and travel. Her children, however, were her salvation. First she had Heather; then she had the baby—two precious little ones. Somehow she endured, albeit rather mechanically, and emerged from that awful first year, then took the strong parenting lead she continued to exhibit throughout the children's formative years. Today she remembers that she was entirely happy with that involvement and during those days. Because she saw the traumatic effect on children when they lose a parent, she endeavored to create a loving, nurturing, comforting, secure environment for her own children. The loss of a parent frightens children: *Dad is gone. What if something happens to Mom?* Quite aware of those fears she worked to prevent them from overcoming her children. The children were well aware of her activity relating to searches for truth about Harley's status, but she kept the home life as normal as possible. She wanted her children to be removed from that controversy and its ensuing emotional toll.

Initially she worked in boutiques; then, when Harley Stephen was in high school and Heather was back East in college, she transitioned to the hospitality industry. She also worked in the medical industry—one she particularly enjoyed. Today she regularly volunteers in a Santa Barbara hospital.

Although her parents lived in Santa Barbara, Mary Lou's childhood home, they often made the four-hour journey to San Diego. The children also often stayed with them, especially when Mary Lou traveled. Heather and Harley Stephen not only loved Grandma and Grandpa but also loved being with them. The grandparents held reciprocal feelings. The only daughter and the oldest of the Marino children, Mary Lou had a special relationship with both her father and her mother. Her father took care of Mary Lou. He gave her financial advice. When Harley had carrier duty or traveled with the Blue Angels, he knew with certainty that Steve would look after Mary Lou and Heather. Because Mary Lou was alone the majority of the few short years she had with Harley, Steve was the only man who consistently watched over her. His death in 1986 was a traumatic loss for not only Mary Lou and her mother but also for Heather and Harley Stephen. He was their surrogate father—the only true male figure regularly present in their lives. For Heather, her grandfather's death hit especially hard. When he died Heather was a high-school senior. At Princeton for her freshman year—far from California and her mother, brother, and grandmother—she did not have family with whom she openly could grieve.

Mary Lou's mom, Minnie Marino, her easy-going personality a contrast to the gregarious, outgoing one of her husband, was gentle and loving. Her quiet strength provided comfort, wisdom, and unending love and nurture. Because of illness she ultimately became unable to care for herself. In 2002 Mary Lou moved to her hometown of Santa Barbara. Although moving back to her hometown allowed her to reconnect with childhood friends and extended family members, she had left her established circle of friends and routines of San Diego. When her mom died in October 2010, Mary Lou knew that the death would be a blessing and absolutely the best thing for her mom, but it still impacted her deeply. She and the Hall children all continue to miss these two loving influences—their grandparents. Mary Lou describes their occasional sad days as a *Grandpa day* or a *Grandma day*. On such occasions she and the children understand each other; nothing more needs to be said.

    Mary Lou felt, and even today sometimes feels, alone. After her mom's death in 2010, this was especially keenly felt. Because she had expected her mother's death, Mary Lou hadn't expect to feel such profound grief—grief partially magnified by her sense of aloneness.
    She describes it: *Harley's gone. I've buried my father. I've buried my mother. I let my children go to their own lives. I insisted they make their own ways and helped them gain their education. I fostered their independence and encouraged them to find careers in which they would be happy and successful. At times now, waves of melancholy surface: I'm so tired. This is all too much. It's gone on too long.*
    When asked how she endured and triumphed through all those years after Harley's shootdown, she's quick to respond: *One doesn't ever get over this loss. It is always with me. I can see Harley standing in the Hong Kong hotel room, see the shirt he was wearing, see him in so many places. Each image is clear, real. That is hard to believe after so many years have gone by, but it is true. The children saved me and are still*

saving me. *I could not have survived or continue to survive without my friends and close family. Bruce Bailey, my CACO, truly cared about me as a person. He and his wife became good friends. He has watched out for me through these many years, as have other friends. When Bruce was killed in an airplane crash, I helped his wife, Nancy, as Bruce had helped me.*

One of the three friends whose husband was POW/MIA from those early years and Mary Lou remain good friends. They see each other often. Unless something unusual prompts the discussion, the two women do not talk about POW/MIA matters or the loss of their husbands. They are no different from any other two women having friendly chats over coffee or sharing family news. Mary Lou also has stayed especially close to Harley's older sister, Kay, and her husband, Bob.

Recently, remains of former POW's and MIA's found in Southeast Asia have been identified, returned, and buried in the U.S. The Paris Peace Accords was signed January 27, 1973—almost 40 years ago. For several years the return of service personnel was the norm, but not some four decades later. As she says, *Return of remains is starting again. This bothers me. Do I expect to open the door to see Harley? No, not Harley. Earlier on many occasions someone, in accordance with military protocol, appeared at my door. That is what has happened recently to these families. They have remains returned after so many years. Did I ever go to Vietnam? No, never. I didn't want to go earlier. I still don't. I have no desire to look for anything there, nor do the children.*

Forthrightly she explains that she truly doesn't know what happened to Harley. Internet articles erroneously have stated that she believes Harley is dead. Mary Lou never has made this statement. With candor, she elaborates: *I'm a realist, though. How many years has it been? It's unrealistic to think he'd be walking down a street in Southeast Asia. I've pictured every possible scenario about his treatment, his fate. But. I. Do. Not. Know. That's the problem. That's why we can't have closure. That's why we can't make peace for Harley.* Her voice is tinged with a plea that we accept the truth of her not knowing.

She continues: *We don't have the peace closure gives. Funerals are for the living and bring closure. We've never had that nor the courtesy of even knowing whether he is dead or alive. I made peace <u>with</u> Harley but not <u>for</u> Harley. Heather and I feel anger—not unhealthy anger but normal anger because we don't have peace; we don't know the answers. The government deliberately left those men there, knowing those men were alive.*

Sometimes I think of Harley and how much I miss him. If only he could see his children! They've done so well. That he has not seen them hurts so much. And my dad is gone. I miss him so. January is a bad month for me. Dad died January 7. Harley was shot down January 27. The spring Heather's acceptance letter from Princeton came, I cried because Dad and Harley weren't there. They've missed all the wonderful things involving the children. Each of those wonderful events has carried a touch of sadness—the acceptance letter, their accomplishments, the truly big things. Then I remember that Harley does know. Dad knows. They both know. But they aren't with us.

Although I was reared a Catholic and Harley a Methodist, those differences didn't matter. Each time we went to see my parents, we attended services at the Episcopal church in which we were married. That Episcopal minister, Dr. George Hall [no relation], *such a great speaker, became a close friend. He often asked Harley to talk with the youth on Sunday evenings. I wish Dr. Hall were still here in Santa Barbara. But I don't have to depend on the church. I depend on God. I do have a strong faith. I'm forever talking to God. In high school I recognized God is a loving God and that I could talk directly to Him.*

Knowing that in heaven I will be with Harley and Dad and Mom gives me great comfort. I do not fear death. I know where I'm going and whom I'm going to see. When the time comes, I will be ready. I'm so anxious to see Harley, my father, my mother.
What strength and assurance Mary Lou exhibits!

Mary Lou, quick to point out that her husband was more than a naval aviator—a giant of a man—directs interviewers to the Virtual Wall dedicated to Harley. An entry by Max Guiley and dated June 19, 2003, she indicates, shows Harley much as he thought of himself—just an ordinary person:

> It was in the late spring of 1972 at VT-4, NAS Pensacola, while a Naval flight student in basic carrier-quals and ACM in the T-2B, when I had the—to me—unbelievably great honor of being scheduled to fly some syllabus training flights with the "funner-than-fun" then-CDR Harley Hall! His coach-like charisma was riveting, and he seemed to continuously be holding an impromptu moving-classroom with him wherever he walked or paused—usually with five or six other guys tagging along, competing to ask questions and intently listening to hear his enjoyably mesmerizing and animated answers.
> He was the absolute epitome of full-of-life enthusiasm and down-to-earth humor—a natural-born teacher who spiced our interest in learning all we possibly could about Naval Aviation just by virtue of his personal example of exquisite flying expertise and the uncanny ability to explain it in terms we college-boys could enjoy and understand.
> As nearly-captured in his photograph here, CDR

Hall was a larger-than-life man's man who had a truly Peter Pan-like, bright-eyed empathy for us green-mere-mortals; and yet, he never flaunted his accomplishments. In fact, when I first began flying with him, Harley Hall won my utmost respect, and I just naturally idolized him, without my even realizing at the time he was the former boss of the "Blues"—I just instinctively sensed I was flying with greatness. I was right.

During one of those walking-classroom sessions of his—this particular "period" concerning Air Combat Maneuvering—CDR Hall solidly showed us his firm grasp of human-nature and reality and his own unabashed humility by laughingly interrupting himself during an explanation of a specific dog-fighting tactic, exclaiming, "Ya' know? We're gonna teach you guys all these fancy ACM techniques, but as soon as you see your first MiG, all this great knowledge will fly right out the canopy glass, and it'll be 'catch-as-catch-can' from then on!"

I shall never forget him nor that day and his statement as long as I live.

Bless you for your always day-brightening sunshine, Mr. Hall, Sir; Godspeed!

With her equanimity and aplomb, Mary Lou moves forward like the indomitable, spirited woman she is. Jim Maslowski, quoted earlier, knew the importance of Harley's service to his country, his dedication to his career, and his devotion to his family. Jim's poignant tribute to his fellow Blue Angel, his mentor, and his friend, as well as this one by Max Guiley, serve not only as a reminder of Hall's efforts on behalf of America, of liberty, of the people's vote, and of family, but also as summaries of the life of Harley H. Hall—the best of the best!

References

A Brief History of US Navy Aircraft Carriers. www.navy.mil/navydata/navy_legacy.

Angel, Mack. Personal interview. 2003.

Anton, Frank. *Why Didn't You Get Me Out?* Arlington, TX: Summit, 1997. 170-183.

"Bamboo Cages, Boils, and Six Years in Solitary." *Newsweek* 12 Mar. 1973: 33.

Beardsley, Bill. Personal interviews. 2002, 2011.

"Beyond the Worst Suspicions." *Time* 9 Apr. 1972. 20.

Blue Angel Video. Producer Duke Vincent. San Diego, 2001. Film.

Blue Angels 1970: U.S. Navy Flight Demonstration Team. U.S. Navy Flight Demonstration Team Publication. 1970.

Bohlen, Christine. *New York Times* 11 Apr. 1993: A1, A13.

Chanoff, David. "The Man Who Knows Too Much." *Boston Magazine* Oct. 1993: 82.

Christensen, Ernest. Personal interviews. 2003, 2011.

Davis, J.D. Personal interviews. 2001, 2002.

Denton, Tommy. "Who Leaked the Classified Information?" Fort Worth *Star-Telegram* 14 May 1992.

Elliott, James, DDS. Personal interview. Fort Worth, TX. 2002.

Garrison, Peter and George Hall. *CV: Carrier Aviation.* Novato, CA: Presidio Press, 1980. 70-74.

Gertz, Bill. *Washington Times* 8 Apr.1993: A5.

Hall, George. *Top Gun.* Novato, CA: Presidio, 1987. 30-33.

Hall, Mary Lou. Personal interviews. 2002, 2011.

Hearings before the Senate Select Committee on POW/MIA Affairs. Nov. 5-7, 15, 1991.

Heath, Terry. Personal interview. 2001.
Hendon, Bill and Elizabeth Stewart. *An Enormous Crime*. NY: St. Martin's, 2007.
Herbert, Frank. *Threshold: The Blue Angels Experience*. The text and full-color photos from the motion picture. New York: Ballantine, 1973.
Kent, David. Telephone interview. 2011.
Knell, Michael E. "Deal Will Build Vietnam Port." *Boston Herald* 16 Jun. 1993: 32.
Lambert, Steve. Personal interview. 2003.
Maslowski, Jim. Personal interviews. 2002, 2011.
McConnell, Malcolm. *Inside Hanoi's Secret Archives*. New York: Simon and Schuster, 1995. 399-403.
McCreary, John. Personal interview. 2004.
Mezzadri, Frank. Personal interview. 2001, 2002.
Mezzadri, Suzanne. Personal interview. 2003.
"MIA Families: Living Death." *Newsweek* 26 Jan. 1974: 69.
Nixon, Richard. "Address to the Nation about Vietnam 29 March 1973." *Public Papers of the Presidents*. Washington, DC: U.S. Printing Office, 1975.
O'Mara, Kevin. Personal interview. 2003.
O'Mara, Mary Russell. Personal interview. 2003.
Powers, F.N. Jr. Forensic Odontologist. 1993.
"POW's: At Last the Story Can Be Told." *Time* 9 Apr. 1973: 19. Print.
Pritchett, Bill. Personal interview. 2002.
Report of The Senate Select Committee on POW/MIA Affairs. Washington, DC: National Archives. 1991, 1993.
Sauter, Mark and Jim Sanders. *The Men We Left Behind*. Washington, DC: National Archives.
Shoemaker, Steve. Personal interview. 2003.
Switzer, Bill. Personal interview. 2003.
Tannenbaum. "Papa Wasn't a Rolling Stone . . . He Was a

'Puking Dog.'" *The Hook* Fall 2001. 26.
"The Ships Named Enterprise." U.S. Navy publication.
Threshold: The Blue Angel Experience. Gardner Marlow. 1974. Film.
USS Enterprise CVAN 65 Cruise Book 1966. Boston: Burdette, 1966.
USS Enterprise Yankee Station CVAN 65 Cruise Book 1968. Marceline, MO: Walsworth. 1966.
"*USS Enterprise* (CVAN 65): The First and Finest Nuclear-Powered Aircraft Carrier." *www.enterprise.navy.mil*.
Veronico, Nicholas A. and Margo B. Fritz. *Blue Angels: Fifty Years of Precision Flying*. Osceola, WA: MBI Publishing, 1996. 11-15.
"Vietnam's 1972 Statement." *New York Times* 11 Apr. 1993: A6.

Photo Album

Harley, 3 years 9 months, with sister Kay, 6

Young Harley

Harley with his prize cow, his 4H project

Harley painting the house, 1953

Playing baseball for Clark College

Cutting the cake with his saber after his August 1965 marriage to Mary Lou

Harley and Mary Lou with Harley's parents, 1969

Mary Lou at a dinner

187

Harley blows a bubble for Heather

Harley with Heather in Pensacola

Harley, holding Heather, climbs into Blue Angel No. 1, his F-4

Mary Lou and Harley with string of trout; fishing in High Sierras, 1972

Cleaning fish—last vacation before Harley left for Vietnam

Heather and Harley, with High Sierras in background

Mary Lou and Harley in Hong Kong, December 1972; last time they saw each other

Harley signs autographs after a Blue Angels' show.

Harley and fellow Blue Angel Jim Maslowski at a formal Navy dinner

Harley signs a report after a flight.

**Blue Angels team members under Harley Hall's command
(see page 11 for team members' titles, years of service)**

Harley Hall

Kevin O'Mara

Jim Maslowski

Ernie Christensen

Steve Shoemaker

Skip Umstead

J.D. Davis

Dick Schram

Bill Beardsley

Bill Switzer

Mack Prose

Mary Russell O'Mara

Jack Keen

Bill Pritchett

Ed Spinelli

189

Blue Angels in their A-4 Diamond formation

1970 Blue Angels autographed photo

1971 Bue Angels autographed photo

Maintenance personnel, 1970 Blue Angels

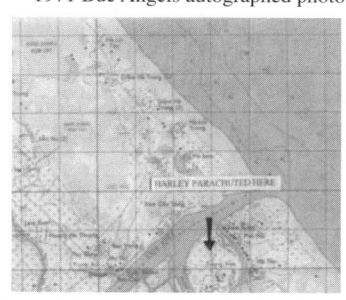

Map of location of Harley's shootdown

Maintenance personnel, 1971 Blue Angels

At left, Heather as a child; center, Heather watches her dad during a Blue Angels air show; right, the Navy Flyer's Creed

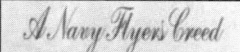

190

Heather and her baby brother, Harley Stephen

Heather, age 14

Harley Stephen, age 15

Harley Stephen sits in a Blue Angel F-4 and gives the traditional pilot's thumbs-up sign as though ready to take off.

Harley Stephen and his mom

As his dad once did, Harley Stephen fishes in the Sierras.

Harley and Arica in their September 2008 wedding

Heather and Arica

Heather

Mary Lou and Harley at his wedding

191